Praise for Jeffrey's books, talks and coaching.

Jeffrey is addressing a critical marketing tactic that is neglected too often by too many contractors. This book is worth reading to help any contractor better leverage their relationships. — **Kevin Kehoe, Consultant**

Energetic delivery, insightful. — **Shawn Sanders, Turf Tenders**

Inspiring and informative. — **John Pontarelli, Proscape**

Jeff brought focus to the muddle. — **Thom Bourne, Ottawa, Canada**

Our company has been focused on direct response marketing in the past and only beginning to place an emphasis on branding the company. Jeff provided a really great framework to build our brand. — **David Chu, GreenLawn Fertilizing**

Jeff made me realize I need to spend time with clients getting to know them better in order to stand out. — **D. Batey, Ruppert Companies**

Good, solid information. This information is easy to apply to our business. — **John Peterson, Wheeler Landscaping**

After learning about branding from Jeff, my existing clients or any future ones will know exactly why I am the company to fulfill their needs. — **S. Ridley, 3D Landscape Group**

Jeff motivated me to improve our client relationships. — **Frank Bango**

Jeffrey's ideas are practical and useful for companies of any size. — **Teresa Croy**

Your customer survey information was eye opening. — **Greg Roemer, A to Z Lawn**

You helped create a more clear and concise strategy about branding and our company image. — **Matt Griffin, Prime Lawn**

Jeff gave a new meaning to "thinking outside the box."
—**Tim, Suncrest Gardens**

I have been motivated to let customers we've had for years know how much we appreciate them, and I need to check on them in person more frequently. This will get them to talk about us. — **Matt Kruse, Ultra Lawn**

Jeff showed me new innovative ways to keep my customer retention high.
— **Kyle Ratcliffe, Dr. Green**

Jeffrey taught me to always remember to think out of the box, have fun, be creative, yet be consistent. — **Craig Kopfmann, Green Acres Landscaping**

Best thing for me today! Get back to basics and show the love. I took over a 25 yr old company that is known for being cheaper and has a lot of older clients. I think I learned everything I needed. It was great!
— **Chuck Morgan, Woburn, MA**

Free Stuff!

A $125 value ... for readers of this book.

For a chance to win a free copy of my next book by sharing your best success story, **see chapter 20.**

For a free marketing calendar, **see chapter 26.**

For a free self-questionnaire that will help you generate breakthroughs in your referral process, **see chapter 33.**

For a free copy of my article "Harvesting Referrals from Realtors,"
see chapter 39.

For a free overview of how peer groups work, **see chapter 43.**

For a free self-audit tool that will help you conduct a referral analysis,
see chapter 63.

For a free tool you can use to determine the ROI of your referral campaigns,
see chapter 74.

For a free overview of the hard and soft qualifiers you can use to evaluate referrals, **see chapter 78.**

For a free tool you can use to stay in touch with referrers and potential referrers, **see chapter 83.**

How Do You ... ?

- Increase referrals from the *trade?*
- *Grow* your enhancement sales?
- Generate referral sales *faster*?
- Pick the *right* incentive programs, avoiding the mistakes?
- Generate more referrals from *high-end* clients?
- Use referrals-systems to make it *easier* in season?

To find out how, read on ...

Jeffrey Scott's

THE REFERRAL
ADVANTAGE

*How to increase sales and grow
your landscape business by referral!*

Contact Jeffrey Scott: 203 220-8931

www.JeffreyScott.biz

jeff@jeffreyscott.biz

Cover design: AuthorSupport.com
Interior layout: ParisiStudios.com
Editorial consulting: iWordsmith.com

Table of Contents

Where Do I Find ...?

INTRODUCTION

Who is Jeffrey Scott?
How to make best use of this book.

I. THE BASICS: IF YOU REMEMBER NOTHING ELSE... REMEMBER THIS!

II. POPPING THE QUESTION: THE ART OF ASKING FOR THE REFERRAL

III. REFERRALS AND YOUR MARKETING PLAN: WHY YOU NEED BOTH

INTRODUCTION

Who is Jeffrey Scott — and why do people listen to what he has to say about generating referrals?

Jeffrey Scott grew referral sales in his landscape and maintenance company by 4000%.

RESULTS COUNT! Jeffrey has over 20 years in the industry and has worked in or overseen most areas of a design, build, maintain, tree, and lawn care firm. When he ran his family's business (www.glengatecompany.com), he grew referral sales from professionals alone, from $50,000 up to $2 million. This was helped by his increasing client retention in one division to 98%.

THE STORY BEHIND THE RESULTS: Jeffrey grew up in both the "blue" (swimming pool) and "green" industries, getting chemicals and dirt under his fingernails by day, and talking to customers at night. When his childhood friends found summer jobs at places like the local ice cream parlor, he worked days and weekends in "the business." After saving his money and going to college, he graduated with a degree in Engineering from New Orleans. He then moved to Europe, where he put himself through business school. He worked hard consulting with European companies on the best ways to grow their businesses. It was during this period while in Holland, that he met his future wife: Corine.

Jeffrey returned to the US, joined his family's business full time, and soon took over its management. After years of growth and innovation at Glen Gate Pool & Property, the urge to continue consulting returned, and he opened Landscape Success Systems. He is now dedicated to helping green-industry companies *captivate the right clients, grow their business, build their wealth, and have more fun in the process.* Learn more at www.JeffreyScott.biz.

THE LEADERS EDGE: As part of his work, he runs THE LEADERS EDGE, a peer program for busy landscape professionals who want to work in a small-group environment, to discuss burning issues and best practices, and learn new ways to grow their business in any economy. For information on THE LEADERS EDGE, or for a free article on how peer groups work, email Jeffrey at referrals@jeffreyscott.biz.

This book is based on 92 questions.

Over the years, in settings such as free teleseminars, coaching meetings, and hallway conversations at association meetings, contractors have asked Jeffrey countless variations on this question: "How do I grow my business by referral?" This book offers the answers to 92 variations on this question.

DEDICATION: Jeffrey does all this for his wife and three children, who have grown accustomed to a lifestyle that includes a busy husband and proud father who adores his family and loves his work. This book is dedicated to them: Corine, Michael, Max and Kate.

How do I make best use of this book?

FIRST AND FOREMOST, DO QUALITY WORK THAT FOLLOWS A QUALITY PROCESS. If you expect to increase your referrals by using the ideas in this book, it will help if your clients are already happy with:

- The quality of your work.

- The process you take them through: from initial contact, to contract signing, to execution.

In this book, you will read a number of ideas for improving your processes and your overall quality. But remember, quality is a mindset. As you read this book, keep the following question in mind: *"Is the quality of my work consistently high — and is it worthy of a referral?"*

SECOND, READ ONE SECTION AT A TIME. Take this book in bite-sized chunks. Don't try to digest it all in one sitting. Try to implement one section (or even one chapter) at a time.

Start with any section you want—choose whichever you think will help you succeed most in your job or at your company. Remember to keep perspective: even if you only implement a third of what you read here, you will still be miles ahead of your competition!

FINALLY, SHARE THE LOAD. Share this book with others. Involve everyone in your company; let your staff read it and discuss the best ideas with each other. Get buy-in by talking in groups about the specific ideas you find here.

Don't try to implement all these ideas on your own—unless you work alone, in which case you should find a trusted friend or business coach to help you discuss and prioritize the ideas.

Adapt the ideas in this book so that they fit your team, your company, and your marketplace. Then set up a plan … and work it consistently!

❶
THE BASICS
If You Remember Nothing Else …
Remember This!

Should my goal be to get 100% of my business from referrals?

You may be surprised that my answer on this is "NO."

SOME REFERRALS NEED A MARKETING PUSH. Obtaining 100% of your business from referrals should NOT be your goal when you hope to *maximize* referrals. To do this requires that you support your referral efforts with some carefully selected marketing initiatives. Together these will maximize not only your referrals, but also increase your non-referral customers. Later in this book you will read more about the profitable "synergy" to be gained by integrating your referral strategies with your other marketing plans.

When I first took aim at increasing referrals at Glen Gate, I focused on increasing both customer referrals and professional referrals. On the professional side, we were receiving approximately $50,000 in work from realtors every year, and I felt we could do a lot better. After all, realtors influence perhaps 80% of all new home-owner decisions when it comes to construction and property care services! So I put together a plan that involved direct mail pieces that told realtors about our services; I combined this with a strategy of making in-person presentations at realtors' offices. At these presentations I promoted evaluation and inspection services that realtors could offer their clients as part of the home-buying process. Moreover, realtors who lived in the area also saw our marketing materials at home, thanks to our local advertising initiatives with homeowners. Over the years, our referral totals from realtors climbed steadily, and in one year, we received realtor referrals worth $2 million!

NEW GROWTH INITIATIVES REQUIRE MORE THAN "JUST REFERRALS."
Generating 100% of your business from referrals should NOT be your goal when you plan on rolling out new products, introducing new services, or entering new territories. By definition, you're going to be receiving fewer referrals in such situations; you may want to include targeted marketing as part of your rollouts.

A BRANDED IMAGE IS PART OF MARKETING. 100% referrals should NOT be your goal when your plan is to create a "branded, professional" image of your company in your community — the better to separate yourself from the "low-priced two guys in a pickup." Your branded image will inevitably drive new work to you, above and beyond any-word-of mouth referrals that come your way.

TAKING YOUR BUSINESS TO THE NEXT LEVEL? 100% referrals should NOT be your goal when you have an aggressive plan to grow your business to the next level; for example, when you want to grow so that you can finance a transition in company ownership, or when you want to create growth opportunities for key staff. You may need more growth than referrals provide in order to take your business to the next phase of its development.

INCREASING YOUR RETURN ON INVESTMENT. 100% referrals should NOT be your goal when you hope to maximize your business's *return on investment.* Generating all of your business from referrals in this situation would mean (for instance) overlooking customers who:

- **SHOP ON THE WORLD WIDE WEB**

- **MAKE "SPONTANEOUS" PURCHASE DECISIONS**

- **MAKE DECISIONS BASED ON WHAT THEY READ, AS OPPOSED TO WHAT THEY HEAR.**

HAVING SAID ALL THAT… I feel strongly that your goal should always be to maximize the natural flow of referrals, regardless of what else you are doing to grow your business. This book is designed to help you do that.

Why do people give referrals? What's in it for them?

The main reason people give referrals is that they like and trust you **PERSONALLY**.

- Not your firm.
- Not your industry.
- Not your boss.
- They give you referrals when they like and trust **YOU**.

Perhaps they feel indebted to you. Perhaps they feel a commonality with you. Perhaps they admire the quality of your work. For whatever reason, you have made a positive connection with them — and in so doing, you have triggered the positive emotion in them that triggers referrals.

In this book, you will learn many ways to make a positive connection happen, and learn how to take full advantage it when it does.

What are referral incentives — and how do I take advantage of them?

Incentives are promises you make to a client or employee in the hope of rewarding that person for doing something for you in return; in this case, bringing you referrals. Sometimes you promise money, sometimes you promise free service, and sometimes you promise a gift.

INCENTIVES WORK WELL IN SOME SITUATIONS AND BACKFIRE IN OTHERS. Incentives should become part of your marketing mix only after careful testing and consideration.

Not all incentive systems work the same, so they must all be tested carefully. Moreover, not all client groups will react the same to incentives; so again, you have to test each of your client groups separately.

REWARDS: Some companies reward with gifts, some reward with free services, and some reward with money. Gifts are the least likely to offend, though free services may be more effective in motivating people to actively hunt down referrals for you. Money is the incentive that requires the most care. In some cases, it works great, but in others it can distract people from your core relationship, or even be viewed as unethical.

Some client groups want no incentives at all – they simply want you to WOW them and service the heck out of them.

I've devoted an entire section of the book (Section IX) to this complex topic. I believe you will make the best decisions about referral incentives once you have read this book all the way through.

Incentives are very powerful — use them, but use with caution.

What's the difference between *homeowner* referrals and *professional* referrals?

While there are differences, referrals will come from anywhere, regardless of the segment of the market you're serving.

ANYONE who meets you, likes you, trusts you, learns about your business and what makes you special, and feels a desire to help you — will create referrals for you if they are able.

This is one of the biggest networking lessons you will learn here:

> Each and every day you leave the house,
> you have the chance to meet someone
> who can send business your way.

There are different techniques you can use to create referrals from these two groups. But the basics are the same.

- Build trust.
- Build a relationship.
- Be someone worth referring.

After that, you can focus on specific tactics, depending on the role this person can play in your business.

This section will provide you with techniques to generate referrals from both groups.

When should I NOT ask for a referral?

When you don't know how the client feels.

In other words, when it is possible that the client is peeved at you or your firm. The problem is, you won't always know when a client is upset with you.

THE TRICK is always to be in contact with your clients, and to inquire constantly about their expectations and their happiness: "Have we met your expect-ations?" This may seem like obvious advice, but I've run into many situations where it is ignored. Uncovering your clients' expectations is an ongoing pro-cess of discovery. Never stop inquiring!

IS THE RELATIONSHIP TOO NEW? You also should not ask for a referral if you have not yet proven yourself and/or established good rapport with your cus-tomer. For example, I once met an insurance salesman who asked me for three referrals the very first time we ever met. I thought to myself, "Are you kidding me?" I'm sure he read about that technique in some old-fashioned sales training book. Not only did he NOT get the referrals — he did NOT get my business!

Keep your priorities straight: Build the relationship. Exceed their expectations. Then get the referral!

HAS SOMEONE ELSE IN YOUR ORGANIZATION BEEN ASKING FOR REFER-RALS? You also should not ask for a referral if someone else from your firm just asked the same person for a referral. The left hand should always know what the right hand is doing!

ARE YOU TERRIFIED? Don't ask for a referral if you are feeling needy or desperate. Such feelings will usually show through. The best remedy for this problem, of course, is to generate so many automatic referrals that you never become desperate. This book will help you avoid that problem. (I've devoted an entire section of this book — Section VII.)

What's the one thing I should remember — if I remember nothing else?

Remember the Rule of Reciprocity.
Put simply, this means YOU GET WHAT YOU GIVE.

When you ask people what kinds of referrals they are looking for, or more simply, what kind of help they are looking for — and if you then offer them help — you will greatly increase your chances of receiving referrals in return.

Whenever I network with another professional, I always ask him or her, "How can I help you?" I do this even when it seems there is nothing in it for me. I met a landscape design expert a while back, and asked him how I could help him. Recently, he emailed me and asked me to help him promote a new design education program he was developing. I was happy to do so, and I did what he asked. I also brainstormed with him about new ways for him to promote his business. I then volunteered to execute one of the ideas we developed.

At that point—after he was absolutely thrilled with me for offering my help— I realized he could help me and so I "popped the question." I asked him for the names of green-industry professionals that might have an interest or need in a peer program I am running. He emailed me names of six friends of his, and he put in a good word for me with each of them. This is what I call the Rule of Reciprocity in action!

THE RULE OF RECIPROCITY connects to most of what follows in this book. Once you learn to see opportunities to help other people as *investments in your own business*, you will be better positioned to maximize your natural flow of referrals.

II

POPPING THE QUESTION

The Art of
Asking for the Referral

Whom should I ask for referrals – and whom should I avoid?

It's a good assumption that clients will refer friends similar to themselves. Thus, you want referrals from your *ideal* clients, clients who belong in one or more of the following groups:

- **LOW-HASSLE CLIENTS.** These people make it easy for you to deliver high value to them. (Of course, not all good clients are low-hassle; some are high-paying high-hassle clients who will push your company to the next level!)

- **HIGH-DOLLAR-VOLUME CLIENTS.** These people make it possible for you to reach your sales goals.

- **HIGH-MARGIN CLIENTS.** These people make it possible for you to reach your profit goals.

- **LIKEABLE CLIENTS.** These are clients who make it fun to do business; clients with whom you have great personal chemistry.

In addition, you want referrals from **INFLUENCERS.**

These are people who have access to your ideal client group, even though they themselves may not be clients. These may be leaders in a garden club, the president of the local builder's council, or a leading member of the Chamber of Commerce. As you make friends with influencers, it is of course possible that they too will become your clients.

AVOID PROBLEM CLIENTS. There are clients who are more trouble than they're worth. I know this from experience.

My firm once received what we thought was a promising referral. The referral told us, "I've worked with two other companies, but I just wasn't happy with them." That should have been our tip-off! This person turned out to be argumentative during the entire sales process, and the project turned out to be the job from H___!

When a client is highly problematic during the sales process, you should expect him or her to be problematic as a client. Focus on the people who want what you are selling, and generate more referrals from that group.

I know a highly successful designer of swimming pools in Arizona who has a very direct and effective way of dealing with this situation. While she's still on the phone, she asks her leads, "Are you a nice person? We only work for nice people." This sets the expectation up front, in a lighthearted manner, that only nice behavior will be tolerated.

CAVEAT: There's a difference between "problematic" and "demanding." Some highly demanding people will actually raise your standards and send you referrals. These people are blessings in disguise. Whereas problematic clients only add to your list of headaches.

THINK GEO-FOCUS: Avoid asking for referrals from those whose contacts fall outside of your geographical area — unless you know that their contacts will be highly lucrative for you. With fuel prices as high as they are, you want to pick your "drive-to spots" carefully.

Tell people exactly what geographic area you're targeting, and you will attract more targeted referrals.

8

Is there a *right time* to ask a client for a referral?

There are many "right times" to ask.

THE "IDEAL" RIGHT TIME to ask for a referral is when you have exceeded someone's expectations, and you know for certain that the client is delighted with your work. This could be at the completion of the project, or at some point where the client is clearly happy with the ongoing maintenance you're performing. You've fulfilled your commitment, and the client has been WOWED and is feeling indebted to you. This is a great time to cash in the positive energy you've built up during the relationship!

THE "ANY-TIME" RIGHT TIME to ask for a referral is when the client is happy with any aspect of your job and starts gushing with compliments. This may happen in the middle of a job, or at any moment in time when you've done something wonderful. At this point, the client may even send you a referral without your asking for one. Keep in mind, on long construction jobs, that it doesn't always pay to wait till the end of the job to bring up the issue of referrals. Clients can get tired of seeing you after so many months of upheaval on their property, and they just want you to go away and leave them alone for a while.

THE "FOLLOW-UP" RIGHT TIME is between six months and a year after you've completed the job — perhaps when you're walking the property with the client, either to maintain it or to visit the site for a complimentary checkup. I do these kinds of visits out of professional pride. At this point, clients are reminded of what a good job you did, and will start to revisit how great they felt about working with you. This is a good time to ask for a referral.

Reconnect to the positive energy you created at the beginning of the relationship.

THE "UNIQUE" RIGHT TIME is any point in the relationship when you've done something unique or special for the client.

We worked with a client who had a rodent problem, and we helped simplify that client's life by having the animal removed. The client was ecstatic. That's when we asked, "Do you know of anyone else who needs help removing wild animals from their property?"

THE "MOMENT OF TRUTH." In general, the right time to ask for a referral is during a "moment of truth." That's a moment when you and your customer are sharing a positive feeling and everything seems to be going right, and you know for sure that you have built up good will. Ask ... but don't abuse the situation by asking for a referral *each and every* time you experience the "moment of truth." Timing is everything. Don't become a pest.

GETTING WITHOUT ASKING: Some people are experts at generating referrals without ever actually coming out and *asking* for the referral. These are the real referral masters. I'll tell you more about what these people do right in later chapters.

The Referral Masters get referrals without
asking for them. Find out who they are,
and make friends with them,
and learn from them.

What do I say exactly, and how do I say it?

There is no single correct way to ask for a referral. Use these examples as models for developing your own referral requests in your own voice.

- "Do you have any friends I should meet who would enjoy the same level of service that you're enjoying?" (Now stop talking — wait for the answer. Then ask, "Would you mind introducing us?")

- "Do you know any neighbors (or know any neighboring businesses around here) that could use our help?" (Stop talking — wait for the answer. Then ask, "Would you mind introducing us?" Or, "Would you mind showing me where they are?" Then go knock on the person's door together.)

- "Does your company have any affiliates that could use our services?" (Stop talking — wait for the answer.)

- "Do you have friends or colleagues who are complaining about their service? (Offer to do an initial consultation with their friends for free.)

I'm particularly fond of the phrase, "Do you have any friends I should meet… ?" This subtly and effectively sets up the fact that you're asking for an introduction.

CAVEAT: Don't pressure people to give you an introduction when they're not comfortable doing so.

I once asked a client if there was anyone he knew that I should meet, and he said "Yes, absolutely" — but he wasn't comfortable setting up an introduction. Two months later, the person he had wanted to refer us called us directly. The customer HAD introduced us — but in his own way, behind the scenes.

PRACTICE: The more often you ask for referrals, the easier it becomes—but don't overdo it with your live prospects and customers! One way to develop the skill is to write down a script that you feel comfortable with. Memorize it. Practice your script twenty times on a friend or colleague. Internalize the script. Then throw it away.

What if I'm not comfortable asking *directly* for a referral?

Sometimes you will be able to slip it into the conversation on the way out the door:

"BY THE WAY … do you know of someone you think might benefit from our service?"

I call this (easy-to-execute) maneuver the Colombo Strategy, after the famous 1970s television detective played by Peter Falk. He always saved his most important question for last, and he usually got a positive reaction because of his low-pressure approach.

ALTERNATIVE APPROACH: You may prefer to ask for a referral by using a set-up question that will make the process easier:

"Is there anything we are not doing that you wish we were?"

This is a great strategy, because it delivers three possible outcomes, each of which has the potential to benefit you.

1. The person may tell you about a problem, which is certainly something you will want to listen to carefully and fix.

2. The person may tell you about another opportunity for work he or she wants done, in which case you're in a great position to sell more services.

3. The person may say that everything is fine — in this situation, you will find it much easier to ask for a referral. (Just be sure he or she is not simply being polite. It helps to ask a few different times, a few different ways, to make sure everything is really fine. I will cover this in more detail in an upcoming chapter).

Are there ways to ask for a referral without seeming invasive?

This is an important question. I know from personal experience that it is possible to be invasive.

I once asked a client for a referral, and I "pushed" the question a couple of steps too far. He wanted to give us a referral, and he eventually did. He just didn't like how I had raised the subject and pursued the referral. Some things have to happen in their own due time. Here are two ways to raise the subject that are a little different from the traditional approaches.

SHARE YOUR GOALS UP FRONT: Tell the customer about your goals when you meet. "Make your goals a selling point: "Our aim here is to do such a good job for you that you will refer your friends and neighbors to us." If you're feeling bold, you add later on: "Will you be willing to refer us after we do a great job for you?" As you are working for the client, ask, "How are we doing? Are we meeting all your expectations?" When you hear a whole-hearted "Great!" in response to that question, and you have built up a trusting relationship, it may be the time to inquire if you are doing well enough to earn the person's referral. (Caveat: this last question can come across as invasive—so you will have to decide on a case-by-case basis when it makes sense to use.)

GIVE TO THE COMMUNITY: A very creative way to take the pressure off is to ask the person to pass along the word about something special you are doing — for instance, raising money for a local charity. This is a great public relations technique that doubles as a referral technique. What client could resist such a request?

If you choose to work with a charity, do so for the right reason: because you really believe in the work the charity does.

Otherwise, your clients and employees will see through your efforts, and you may actually end up doing more harm than good.

Imagine how you would feel saying the following to your clients: "My company is raising money for breast cancer. For every person who writes out a $50 check to breast cancer, we will plant a beautifully pruned ornamental tree in their yard. Would you be willing to pass this information on to your neighbors?" This is a question that any employee would feel proud to ask. What's more, your client will feel proud to brag about you as their service company.

This referral strategy produces a five-way win.

1. You built a positive reputation with the people at your local charity.
2. You can send out a press release to your paper, to ask them to spread the word.
3. Your employees feel good about working for their company.
4. Your clients get into the habit of bragging about you to their neighbors.
5. You physically meet new prospects!

<blockquote>
The universe gives to the givers,
and takes from the *takers.*
Be a *giver.*
</blockquote>

What should I do right after I ask for a referral?

Keep your mouth closed.

LET THE PERSON THINK. Don't break the silence. Give the person time to think — either silently or talking out loud. Sometimes, your silence will lead the person to ask you a clarifying question. Or perhaps the person will bring up a nagging issue or question that has been on the "back burner."

Rule number one is be quiet … and let the other person take the next step.

Once you've made your request, filling the silence with long monologues about how great they are or how wonderful you are, will distract the other person.

Silence is golden.

When you're uncomfortable "riding out" the silence, try counting silently to distract yourself, "one thousand one, one thousand two …" and so on, until you reach ten. If you feel the need to talk, ask some variation on the same question. Then pause again and let the other person answer.

Asking for referrals is like selling. And selling requires good listening. And good listening requires letting the other person talk.

So be quiet, and let the other person think and talk.

How do I know when I've *crossed the line* when asking for a referral?

This depends on the person.

LISTEN: The first thing to do is listen for signs that will tell you how big a priority your contact is willing to make generating referrals for you. Then ... just follow along.

Sometimes "crossing the line" means offering an inappropriate kind of compensation for a referral. Many industries have a code of ethics that prohibit professionals from giving referrals, let alone from taking incentives. **For example:** In Connecticut, home inspectors are not allowed to give referrals at all—and real estate agents, to avoid favoritism, must give three referrals rather than singling out any one vendor. Check the laws in your state and the code of ethics of the professionals in your state. (You will find more on incentives in Section IX.)

PUT THE SHOE ON THE OTHER FOOT. How would you feel if one of your vendors asked you for a referral? What would constitute "crossing the line" for you? Answer this question for yourself, and consider using your own response as a guide.

In the end, each person has his or her own definition of what constitutes crossing the line.

The only way to know for sure what's appropriate with a given person is by maintaining a close relationship with that person.

Is it a good idea to mail a postcard asking for a referral?

It is a great idea to mail your clients periodically throughout the year.

The question is: what should you mail them?

ADD VALUE: Mailing a request for referrals is not the best strategy. You need to mail your clients something that ADDS VALUE to their day. Your mailings should:

- Focus on their needs, and create the desire in them to call you back.
- Provide value by offering a product or service they might need.
- Build up relationships between you and your customer.
- Educate them on issues relevant to their property needs and your services.

FOR EXAMPLE: You can give your customers a reason to call you, by sending a postcard that announces a new "organic" program or offers a discount on a new tree care program. This 'new information' gives them a reason to talk to you or about you, even when they do not buy that particular service from you. I have gotten referrals from prospects that spoke to a salesperson at my company, but never engaged us. Treat everyone you speak with as a potential client, and every potential client as an *actual* client, and you will grow the number of people that advocate for your firm.

Periodically mail your customers information that makes THEM — not you — feel good.

Generally, a referral is something you ask for in person — or perhaps remind people about indirectly in a newsletter, by announcing referrals that others have given your company.

Earning referrals is a step-wise process. Earn their trust, build on that trust when you mail them, and ask for a referral in person.

Can I send a personalized letter asking for a referral?

Personal letters are not for *taking.*
Personal letters are for *building.*

Personal letters are for building relationships and building goodwill. I'm all in favor of personalized letters. These days, they are an opportunity to stand out in the person's mind!!

Examples of reasons to send a letter:

- Thanking the person for the opportunity of working with him or her.
- Sending along a clipping of something of interest to your client.
- Passing along greetings at holiday times.
- Sending a copy of a book you know the person will enjoy.

The point is: you should never ask for a referral in a personal letter, but rather use the letter to give something first. Remember the Rule of Reciprocity.

You can use a letter to set up a later phone call or visit, during which time you can make the referral request. Think of the process of generating a referral as planting a seed and tending it over time. Mailing a personalized letter is like watering the seed; harvesting is best done in person.

Will a customer satisfaction survey generate referrals?

On their own, surveys typically do not generate referrals. But a survey IS part of the process of obtaining a referral.

PERSONAL SURVEY. I learned about a new "personal survey" approach from David Zerfoss, President of Husqvarna Forest and Garden Co. According to David, the key to this approach is to ask your customer the following question in person:

"On a scale of 1 through 10: How likely are you to refer my company to someone you care about?"

After the customer rates their likelihood, you ask him or her what prompted that score. The person will then share with you why he or she gave you the score they did. This approach does two important things for you. First, it gives you the information you need on how to turn this customer into a happy customer. Second, it communicates to the customer in no uncertain terms that you are looking for referrals. (More on this system can be found in the book by the person who developed it: *The Ultimate Question*, by Fred Reichheld.)

Husqvarna routinely uses surveys. Regular contact with dealers and customers ensures that they are able to obtain the feedback needed to continue providing best-in-class products and services — and it allows them to improve on items that require attention. These guys take it to the streets; in David Zerfoss's words:

"This year, we embarked on a President to President tour to 26 markets around the U.S. where I met with the presidents of dealerships across the country. I heard first-hand from them about their concerns about the industry, what they are learning from customers and what we can do to help them continue to operate successful businesses. This is the best example of a live survey process. These independent dealers appreciate the commitment to not just meet with them, but to listen to their concerns and act upon them. It's a business model that we firmly believe in."

PAPER SURVEYS HAVE FLAWS. The customer survey is best done in person or on the phone, not on paper. I recommend the face-to-face method (over paper surveys) for a couple of reasons. First, with a paper survey, you won't learn all the details of why people are unhappy or how you could improve. Only your most articulate customers will take the time to give you this kind of detail in writing. Second, whenever people give you a score of 10, you will have the opportunity to ask them straight away for a referral!

Customer surveys are best done "live" to create maximum value for your company.

ALTERNATIVES. If you don't feel comfortable using this specific "personal survey" system, you may want to follow the concept of simply connecting face-to-face with customers to ask for feedback—especially with your most important clients.

Recently I asked a customer how he thought we were doing, and learned that he was ecstatic with our services. He told me all the reasons he loved us, and how we simply had to "keep on doing" the great things we were doing, and he would remain our customer (for life!). It was at this point that I asked him for a referral. It was the perfect segue!

Do I really need to ask for referrals "in person"?

Only when you want to obtain more referrals.

Let me be clear here — "in person" means voice-to-voice or face-to-face. "In person" is not, however, an e-mail message. In this day and age, e-mail is so easy to use that it's likely to encourage you to say things in a way that could be misinterpreted by the receiving party. Most of us have sent out "quick e-mails" that we wish we hadn't sent.

E-mail, voice-mail, text messaging, and other forms of media are good for building up the relationship … but not as good when it comes to asking directly for referrals. You will do better by talking to people about this on the phone, and even better by meeting them in person.

When you ask, you should be able to see and hear the person's response. Tone and body language are essential parts of the person's emotional response to your request. If you hope to secure a commitment, you will need to be able to "read" the entire message the person is sending you … and have a back-and-forth conversation based on that message.

Is it too bold to ask clients to mention our company's name during their conversations with others?

The answer is YES, it is too bold if YOU are the one broaching the idea.

The answer is NO, it is not too bold if YOUR CLIENT broached the subject first and you are merely following up.

A better strategy is simply to ask for an introduction. When you're bound and determined to have people talk about you when you're not there, the best way to pull this off is the old-fashioned way: Give them something good to talk about!

FOR EXAMPLE: My dad once had a repairman come to his house; the repairman used a drop cloth on the driveway underneath his vehicle to avoid leaving oil stains. Then he laid a second drop cloth at the front door as he entered the house, to avoid tracking dirt into the house. My dad loves telling this story; he is still talking about the "double drop cloth" experience years later.

Don't *ask* clients to talk about you; instead give them a reason to talk about you.

Should I ask for a referral from a prospect even when I don't get the job?

You can, but bear in mind that there are BIGGER opportunities to pursue here than "just a referral."

Think of each prospect as a client that will buy from you at some point in the future. Your job is to build and nurture that relationship.

To nurture a relationship, focus on helping the other person fulfill his or her wants and needs (in keeping with the Rule of Reciprocity.) Think of the classic movie *Miracle on 34th Street*. Do you remember the scene where the Macy's Santa Claus starts referring people to Gimbels, a competing store — and it starts an uproar? That's the spirit you should embody. Keep your goals aligned with your potential client's goals.

To get in this frame of mind, think of yourself as a consultant – and help them make the right choice and thus make yourself invaluable to them. Show them that you are an industry leader, through your knowledge and your willingness and ability to help them.

Some prospects will tell you they cannot use you just yet, but want to use you next year. At this point, you can ask for a referral IF you sense that you have built an exceedingly strong enough relationship with this prospect and deposited enough into the relationship bank.

If you haven't built up enough trust, then continue in your consultant role, and wait for the relationship to ripen

What should I do *right now* to put the ideas in this section into action?

FIND OUT WHO IS LIKELY TO REFER YOU. Write down the names of your top ten clients and commit to checking in with them over the next week.

Call and set up a time to visit with them, either on their property, or at their workplace or for a meal.

If they do not have time to visit in person, then take time over the phone to assess their happiness with your services.

Once you and your client have reconnected, whether on the phone or in person, ask your client, "How likely are you, on a scale of one to ten, to refer me to someone you care about?"

For those that give you a nine or less, take some time to gently explore the reasons behind the score, and find out what you need to do to raise their satisfaction with you to a perfect 10. Your job is then to take care of those issues.

For those that score you a perfect 10, ask for an introduction to someone who can use your services. If the person gives you a name and number (as opposed to an in-person introduction) ask your contact to call that person ahead of time to introduce you, before you follow up with your call.

LET ME KNOW HOW IT WORKS. I invite you to email me your success stories from using this tactic. The best success story I receive wins a free copy of my next book! E-mail me at Referrals@JeffreyScott.biz. Put the words "Success Story" in the subject line.

REFERRALS AND YOUR MARKETING PLAN

Why You Need Both

Will I ever obtain so many referrals that I don't need to invest in marketing?

Only if you are in (what I call) the "milking" phase of your business. In other words, only when you are no longer investing for strong growth, but you are now in the "reaping-what-you-have-sown" mode.

It is a fallacy to think a company doesn't need to market its business simply because referrals are high. To the contrary, your marketing investments will actually promote —and increase — referrals. (That's called synergy!)

There are a number of unfortunate fallacies about referrals that have spread in the green industry. Here are three that connect to this question:

FALLACY 1. *"If I have enough referrals, I don't need to worry about branding my business."*

Wrong! Uniforms, trucks and job signs will always be a part of your marketing world. They are important when it comes to creating a consistent message, and portraying a professional image. A professional, coordinated-looking image will create leads and referrals for you. The resulting revenue from this is what I call the "low hanging fruit" in your marketing and branding plan. Don't ignore it. Take advantage of it.

FALLACY 2. *"All a prospect needs is a strong referral from a friend or associate to be persuaded to hire me."*

I learned that this was a fallacy from direct experience. I had an in-depth conversation with a client after she had spent over $100,000 with my firm. I asked her how she decided to use us, and her response included talking to a referral — but it also included other positive impressions.

First she saw an advertisement…then she saw our trucks…then she got a referral…then she decided to call us…then she got a prompt call back from the right person in our company…then we made a strong impression on our first appointment … and the list goes on and on, up to the point where we brought her a contract and she signed it, without shopping us around.

Clearly, our entire sales process was key in gaining her confidence—and the referral played an important but supporting role in the process.

Marketing plays a significant role in establishing credibility, and directly supports your referral process.

It takes up to 21 positive impressions before a client feels confident enough to give you his or her money.

I read that this concept of *21 impressions* came from a study done by the American Management Association. Your results may vary—but I have found that this concept holds true. Your client is making multiple judgments about your firm over time, as he or she figures out whether to hire you. It is a process that they go through, that you can greatly influence. Good salesmanship is not luck. It is a well-orchestrated process!

FALLACY 3. *"I don't need to market to my existing clients."*

Actually, your customers are among the most important reasons for you to keep investing in marketing. Keep in mind that your company is changing and growing over time. You need to keep communicating with the marketplace about what you're doing and how you are helping to solve your customers' evolving needs. Marketing to current customers will keep you top of mind with them — which is critically important when it comes to them generating referrals for you.

Marketing and referrals work together to create explosive growth — especially when you take a twelve-months-a-year approach to marketing your business. The more consistent your marketing execution is over the span of the year, the more momentum you will gain in both referrals and marketing-based growth.

We already visit my best client's property every month — isn't that enough marketing to generate a referral?

It might be … but you may be leaving money (and referrals) on the table.

Referrals are the result of great relationships, not just great work performed by your company.

WHO IS VISITING? A lot depends on who is visiting the property, and how much expertise and authority that person has.

- How good is that person at initiating dialogue and building rapport?
- How good is he or she at planting seeds for future work?
- How empowered is he or she with time and money to delight your customer?
- Is the person task-oriented or relationship-oriented?

At the end of the day, your company needs to make sure your customer is fully educated in what your company is able to do for them. Who will do this? The person visiting the property?

I HAVE FOUND THE FOLLOWING TO BE TRUE. The fact that our staff had a good relationship with clients didn't mean our customers understood or were buying the full complement of our services! It was only after we made a concerted effort to educate our staff, and asked them to create stronger relationships with our customers, that we improved our cross-selling efforts between our divisions. With this enhanced cross selling, we grew our revenue and grew the number of customers who were referring our larger range of services.

MULTIPLE IMPRESSIONS: Remember — your customers need to be receiving multiple positive impressions of your firm over time, in order to be reminded of the good decision they made hiring you, in order to refer you, and in order to buy more from you.

Each individual customer is different, and each needs to be communicated with in an appropriate way. One marketing piece won't fit all customers. Some want phone calls, some want emails, some want snail mail, some want the solid eye contact and the firm handshake. Some want all of these. That means you not only need multiple impressions, but multiple impressions via different channels.

It pays off:

STATISTICALLY, in my old company, a lead from a current customer to do more work on their property, was, on average, worth six times more in sales, than a lead from a referral. (Are you tracking your leads so you know which is worth more? We will cover more about this in Section XI.)

The lesson is clear: It pays to focus your efforts on your current customers, because they will bring you both referrals and highly valuable upsales!

How do I use my *website* to generate more referrals?

There are different ways to use your website to generate referral sales, and sales in general.

Keep in mind, your website is more likely to be something people will check out AFTER receiving a referral.

Here are examples of ways to use your website to create more referrals, close more referrals, and capture the attention of more web surfers:

OPTIMIZE YOUR WEBSITE so it is more likely to "convert" both the casual web user and the serious shopper. These next four ideas are key to your website's success.

1. Your website address should be easy to remember and spell.

2. Your website should be registered with all the prominent search engines (such as Google and Yahoo) as well as with local online directories.

3. Your company's home page should prominently show:

- Your phone number.
- The area where you work.
- The years in business when significant.
- What you do, using attractive photography.
- And the benefits of hiring you!!!

4. Your company's home page should feature a clear call to action, so that once you hook people, you don't lose them! In fact, all your pages should have a call to action—web customers won't always land on your home page when they're surfing the web.

GIVE YOUR PROSPECTS A REASON TO RETURN TO YOUR WEBSITE.

5. Put useful tips on your website that focus on the problems faced by your ideal prospects. (This assumes that these prospects have the time and inclination to look for answers on your site—not all of them will.)

6. Put articles and archives on your website. This may give your clients a reason to return to your site and possibly share your website with their friends, and it won't hurt your own sales, either.

7. Give people the opportunity to sign up for an e-newsletter, so you can stay in touch with them and increase your chances of closing more business, repeat sales and referrals.

8. Where appropriate, include technical explanations of your services.

PUT PICTURES OF YOUR CLIENTS' PROPERTY on the website.
(Get permission first.)

9. Use photographs to build credibility. A good picture really is worth a thousand words. (A bad picture is also worth a 1000 words—but the words won't be flattering!) Make sure to use high quality photographs that show a finished looking landscape, unless you are showing a "during" or "before and after" comparison. Hire a professional to shoot your best work. When the photos give a client strong bragging rights, don't be surprised when that client e-mails the link to their business contacts, friends, or family.

USE TESTIMONIALS on your website that feature your clients' names.
(Get permission.)

10. Not only will this build credibility, it will also improve your company's Internet profile. When people are doing Google searches on your clients, your website will pop up.

PUT A REFERRAL CORNER on your website that allows your customers to refer other people to your business.

11. I have seen many websites that do this; some even tell you the incentive you will win when the referral is successful. I can't guarantee success with this technique, but depending on your niche, you may decide that it is worth testing.

There are many techniques here and you don't have to use all of them, at least not right away. The first 4 are key, and the rest will depend on your company's strategy. First make sure you have the basics done, and then pick another strategy to try. The web can be overwhelming, so do this one idea at a time, and see what works for you.

If you are redesigning your website, then work with someone who understands both "websites" and "marketing strategies". Many website developers don't come with both expertises. *Caveat Emptor* – which is Latin for "buyer beware" i.e. don't believe everything you are told, and shop around.

It pays to talk to a few different website designers before you decide who you are going to hire. You may be tempted to hire a family member or close friend. Do yourself a favor, and get three proposals before you decide. At the very least, you will become better educated about your options.

What marketing strategies do I use to generate referrals (and sales) from my past customers?

This question implies that you a have a large client base, and you may have fallen out of touch with some of your past customers. The answer is straightforward:

Mail, Write, Call, Visit!

MAIL: They should be receiving mailings from you and your firm; newsletters, postcards, special offers, and so on. Send a postcard or a newsletter. By the way, paper newsletters are much more likely to be read, and are harder to delete, than virtual newsletters.

WRITE: They should be receiving personalized hand-written notes from you. Tell them how much they mean to you.

- Send a birthday card.

- Send a card welcoming the spring.

- Send a card commemorating the anniversary of when you started working together.

- Send a New Year's card (instead of a Holiday card; they will save your New Year's card for months if you write it personally and with emotion. Your Xmas card, on the other hand, will not get more than a 3 second peak, and it will be tossed away unceremoniously.)

Use a tickler system to remind yourself of these critical anniversaries, or write them up ahead of time.

CALL: You can call your customers just to say 'Hi, is there anything I can do for you?' Or call when you are in their neighborhood and you have time to stop by their property. Or call to set up an appointment for a formal walkthrough.

VISIT. Stop by and visit, either with an appointment or unannounced. These visits may take the form of "pre-emptive" warranty visits, or post-job "checking up on my baby" visits, or routine "quality assurance" visits. When you don't manage to meet your client in person, leave a note and place a phone call afterwards.

When you finally connect, be prepared to introduce your client to new services that he or she may need for the property. If your client has bought everything you sell, then develop brand new services. Your clients have an unending supply of problems and needs. (Who doesn't?) Your job is to uncover their needs and communicate effectively how you can solve them.

Consider the concept: renewal and reward

Find a reason to reconnect: a sports game, or a barbecue you're throwing (even one at your own home with your family). Whatever you do, reawaken the relationship. This will improve your chances of getting referrals.

HAVE YOU HAD THIS EXPERIENCE WITH A CLIENT? One of our clients recently was divorced, and she now had to manage her own finances. She was shocked at what she now had to pay for full property care. She was very well off (from the divorce) but she now had to make her own decisions and be responsible for her own future. She soon started complaining about our prices. She loved the service, she loved her property, but she didn't love the cost. She complained throughout the year and into the winter; when it was time to renew, she was hesitant.

HERE IS HOW WE HANDLED IT. It was about that time that we had invited 20 clients and their friends on a personal tour of the Philadelphia Flower Show. We took everyone to the show by bus, gave them a personalized tour and explained how the judging worked. We served wine and cheese on the way home. This newly divorced client brought one of her friends along. By the end of the day, her friend was telling her how lucky she was to have us taking care of her property. When the client got off the bus, she gave us a hug, and told us to come by the next day and she would be happy to sign her agreement.

We renewed the relationship and took it to a new level—and we impressed the heck out of her friend as well. (Her friend happens to be the head of the local garden club.)

Can I use "promotional" marketing items to generate referrals?

The short answer is YES, when you use them to stay "top of mind" with your customer or tradesperson or influencer.

Promotional items are also useful in helping you generate meetings; like all good pieces of marketing, they do double duty.

Effective promotional items come in a few different categories:

- **Traditional "tchotchkes"** featuring your business contact information, such as refrigerator magnets, calendars, coffee mugs, and other "three-dimensional" marketing materials.
- **Higher value items,** such as shirts, utility knives, fancy clocks, etc.
- **Unique larger items** — such as gardening tools, coolers, golf gear and large beach towels.

THE ADVANTAGE of using traditional three-dimensional marketing, like pens and calendars, is that they're inexpensive, and it's easy to order hundreds or even thousands at a time.

THE DISADVANTAGE of these "tchotchkes" is that people will find reasons to throw them away. You might consider going "nontraditional" in search of higher value and more unique ways to stand out. **For instance**, I once received a branded cooler from a magazine in which I advertise. My wife has used it every summer for the past eight years. It was small, and couldn't have been all that expensive, but we still use it all the time.

Here are two tips anyone can use. I learned the following from a friend who is a master at promotions:

1. PROMO ITEMS AS AMMUNITION. Once a relationship with a referrer is established, provide him or her with a supply of promotional items that they can hand out to as a way to help generate referrals. For this purpose use small lightweight items, or, ideally, higher-end items that are functional and have high-perceived value. Of course, these items must be imprinted with a logo, phone number, or website address.

2. GIVE TWO GIFTS. When attending a business meeting, a person seeking referrals may decide to bring along two of the same high-value promotional items, one for the person that he or she is meeting with and the other for that person to give away. Most people will pass along the second item to another person … as long as the item has high-perceived value!

Here's the test for whether your gift is a good promo item: Does the recipient look the item over in detail and say "WOW!"?

If not, the item could actually detract from your reputation.

What should I do *right now* to put the ideas in this section into action?

Set up a marketing calendar.

Create a calendar for all your marketing efforts—both internal marketing aimed at customers and external marketing aimed at new prospects.

EXISTING CUSTOMERS: You should be marketing at least quarterly to existing customers. I recommend, at a minimum:

- Promoting a combination of seasonal services (something aimed at the winter, fall, spring, or summer), and

- Cross-selling services from different divisions in your company (e.g., selling services from your irrigation division to clients in another division).

On top of this, of course, existing customers should be receiving personal notes from their key contact at your company: birthday cards, New Year's cards, and so one. Set all this up ahead of time on your calendar, and spread it out so you don't become overwhelmed. Consistent execution is key!

FOR EXTERNAL PROSPECTS, I recommend setting up a plan over the winter, to be executed throughout the year. Pick either a simple media (perhaps a postcard) or a more complicated media (perhaps a letter and card in an envelope), and put the message out there multiple times. It is best to keep the message the same, and repeat it over and over, until it starts to catch people's attention.

People need to read your message approximately seven times before they focus on, and understand, what you do.

SAMPLE MARKETING CALENDAR. Would you like an example of a Marketing Calendar? I'll send you one if you email me your request at Referrals@JeffreyScott.biz and put "Marketing Calendar" in the subject line.

Ⅳ
DEAL BREAKERS
Overcoming Obstacles to Referrals

What's the single *biggest* obstacle I face in generating referrals?

Your biggest obstacle is YOURSELF!

(Assuming your work is referral-worthy.)

If you are having trouble with referrals, you may be holding yourself back by not connecting with your customers on a personal level, and by not asking for referrals when you do connect. What stops people from taking the right steps?   Usually, it is FEAR. Fortunately, there are ways to overcome your fear. Consider the following:

YOUR PASSION: Take a moment to remind yourself why you originally got into this business. Connect back to your passion! Think clearly about WHY you love what you do. By the way, if you don't love what you do — then find a new position. Love of work will make you outrageously successful. Without it, you won't generate referrals.

YOUR VISION: If you are a business owner, clarify your vision for your company. What do you want your business to look like five years from now? What are you doing today to move your business in that direction? Your best customers WANT you to succeed, and they want to know how they can help you reach your goals. Therefore you need to know where you are going — so you can tell them!

YOUR PERSPECTIVE: Fear of asking for referrals is similar to fear of speaking in public. To overcome this fear, think in terms of serving the customer, rather than serving yourself. This is how I overcome my own stage fright. Each time I prepare to stand up in front of a group, I overcome my fear by directing my brain to focus on the audience's needs: Why are THEY here, what do they need, and how can I help them? It's the same when it comes to asking for referrals. Focus on your customers' interests and on serving them, and it will feel more natural to you when you ask them, "Who else can I serve?"

YOUR TIMELINE: Keep your perspective focused on the long term. Recognize that you're planting seeds, and seeds take time to grow. You will not always get referrals every time or right away. Plant the seed, and water it, and you will reap a benefit.

Building a referral-based business is a marathon, not a sprint.

CREATE YOUR OWN "REFERRAL MISSION STATEMENT" Take some time to write down your passions, your vision for your company or department, and exactly what you do that makes you worth referring.

Identify three new ways you can demonstrate your passion to your customers.... and look for ways, each morning, to live the attitude that you are worth referring.

I keep asking for referrals, but not receiving them. What's wrong?

REALITY CHECK: Take a long, hard look at your company. How's your service?

- Are you doing a COMPLETE job — or leaving small parts undone?

- Is your quality worth referring, from your client's perspective? HOW DO YOU KNOW? Have you asked them?

- Are your customers receiving everything they BELIEVE they contracted? Again, how do you know?

- Is your service UNIQUE, compared with other service companies in your area? Is it actually worth referring? Once again, how do you know?

- Is your service MEMORABLE (in a positive way)? Do the things that you do stick in your customers' minds?

- Do you surprise your clients by going ABOVE AND BEYOND the contract?

- Is what you're giving your client as good as, or BETTER than, what they've experienced from your competitors? (…and again, HOW DO YOU KNOW?)

- Are you focusing on the parts of your client's property that are PRIORITY to them? …and how do you know?

- Is your passion for what you do readily apparent to your customers? Are you personally worth referring?

Are you someone who shows passion and goes above and beyond the call of duty — on a personal and a professional level?

When you lack overflowing passion in your work, your customers STOP referring you.

I have a lot of passion for what I do, but I just don't get enough referrals — how come?

Consider the following possibilities.

IS THERE A PROCESS PROBLEM? Your product and quality may be great, and your enthusiasm may be high, but your process may be PAINFUL for your customers.

Has your client ever had situations where …

- … the schedule isn't met?
- … the job drags on too long?
- … you show up or leave erratically?
- … you pull people off the job temporarily?
- … you issue unanticipated, unexplained, or overcomplicated billing statements?

Do they love you — but hate your process?

IS THERE A COMMUNICATION PROBLEM? Your communication challenges may be your customer's fault – but it doesn't matter, it is still your problem.

Have you become a "desk jockey?" This is something that can creep up slowly in your work style; and before you know it, your communication becomes less personal, less timely, and less frequent.

Have others become go-betweens for you in your relationships with your customers (or worse, your employees)? Yes, it is important to delegate and build up your organization, but as Ronald Reagan once said, you must "trust — but verify."

In the customer service world, this means "delegate, but stay in touch." Or, as my accountant always says, "You need to INspect what you EXpect.

GOT "PEBBLE-IN-THE-SHOE"? You may have left the customer with a small nagging problem. This is either something you knew needed fixing but didn't, or it could be a problem you didn't know about but should have uncovered. The way to address this is to make sure you ask your clients frequently about their satisfaction. Many of us ask the client if there's a problem once, and then think we've done our job! We haven't. There's a Japanese saying that translates as follows: You need to ask an important question five times, five different ways, in order to reach a meaningful answer. You must be ready to do that if you expect to remove all the pebbles in your customers' shoes!

ASK FIVE TIMES: Ask your client how things are going, in different ways, from different angles, with different emphases.

"Is there anything more that we can do?"

"Are there any little things on the property that need to be taken care of?"

"How do you feel everything is going?"

"Have you gotten any feedback from (your spouse/your boss/other managers in the company) that we should be aware of?"

"Do you have any feedback for us before we move on to the next part of the job?"

"Is there anything we should do better?"

"Are there any small things nagging you?"

What will *permanently kill* my chances of obtaining a referral?

Ignoring your client's requests to fix specific problems. Even when you feel they are not your problems or not your fault, you must still fix them if you expect a referral from this person.

NO MATTER THE COST? Even when the costs seem high, you are usually better off — for the sake of reputation and referrals — simply fixing the problem.

DON'T MAKE THIS MISTAKE: On one of our jobs, the client had insisted we use their mason on the job, against our recommendation. We did — and the mason caused a problem, and the clients were now unhappy with the mason's quality. They wanted it fixed. We tried explaining how the client's decisions created this problem, but that only made things worse. The husband and wife who had contracted with us simply wanted the problem to be our responsibility, and they wanted it fixed. Period.

The story gets worse.

When we didn't act fast enough, they started assembling a LAUNDRY LIST of perceived problems with the job. The cost — to us — of solving the problem grew steadily. They held back all payments, and we ended up having to initiate a lawsuit. In the end, we got partial payment — and we STILL had to go back and fix the original problem with the masonry!

JUST DO IT: Obviously, this client didn't refer us to anyone. It would have been a great deal easier and less costly for us to have simply fixed the client's initial problem. If we had done that, we might have won a referral.

I have a customer who *repeatedly* tells me he's going to give me a referral, but nothing ever happens. What's going on?

If it's a real opportunity, the client will give you the person's name, or tell you something about the person. When that's not the kind of information you're hearing, this may be a signal that there's some other issue at hand. The issue could be innocuous — or it could be serious — or it could be unfortunate.

INNOCUOUS: The person may simply be saying this just to make you feel good. He or she has no actual referral to pass along. Don't worry about it.

SERIOUS: The person may be trying to capture your attention, and is using the possibility of a referral to motivate you to do something you ought to be doing anyway. There is a problem in this person's mind. Solve the problem now, and worry about the referral later.

UNFORTUNATE: The person may be trying to convince you to do extra work for free. Separate the issue of the referral from the work at hand. Once you understand what's really going on, you'll be able to make intelligent decisions about what you should charge for and what you shouldn't. My vote is that you get paid for the work you actually do — and take the referral piece out of the equation.

FOR EXAMPLE: A few years back, we had a client who was always telling us how she was referring us in her job as a realtor, but nonetheless she always seemed to be complaining about the services we were performing. In the end, we could not make her happy — she didn't want to spend enough money to take care of her whole place, but she wanted her whole place to look meticulous. We had to forgo the possibility of future referrals, because we were unwilling to *play along with her.*

Keep in mind: if this realtor had really given us referrals, we would have bent over backwards. But she never actually did bring us a referral for as long as we had a relationship with her.

Over the years, I've learned that it is a red flag when people tell me "I'm always referring you."

Generally, if they are always referring me, then I should know these people and already be doing business with them on a constant basis. If I don't really know them, yet they say they are always referring me—then this is too good to be true.

If it sounds too good to be true, it probably is.

Can I repeatedly ask a client for a referral without wearing out my welcome?

You can feel comfortable repeating your request for a referral — PROVIDED that you have recently "raised the bar" with this client, and given the client a new reason to say "WOW!"

This should be a whole new "WOW!" — a wow that operates at a previously unimagined level. You need to make your client think, "Gee, I knew I loved your company, but based on you how you just WOWED me, I now love what you guys do even more!"

The number of referrals you receive over time from someone is ultimately connected to the quality and intensity of your relationship with that person.

It's hard to keep raising the bar, but it's worth the effort — because you can ask for, and earn, a referral with each new level of "WOW!" you reach.

HERE IS HOW I DO IT. I make a point of doing the following in my business. After someone gives me a referral; I look for ways to add even more value into my relationship with that person. I spend extra time, and do something extra for them, or I brainstorm with them about something they need help with, where I could add some unique value. They appreciate that I am spending time thinking about ways to help them.

FOR EXAMPLE: I have given clients a free seminar for their staff; I have also reached out and coached some of their senior employees on key business and personal issues that, at the time, were creating obstacles to growth.

Raise the bar on yourself, and everyone wins.

What should I do *right now* to put the ideas in this section into action?

Identify the two biggest obstacles you face in increasing your company's referrals — and create an action plan for resolving them.

WRITING CREATES COMMITMENT!

Writing down your thoughts and working through your alternatives is the best way I know to identify solutions and create commitment in your mind.

When you articulate the problem and its possible solution — to yourself or others — you are halfway to solving your problem.

Personally, I often don't have the time or patience to sit and write out my thoughts, but when I do, I am always rewarded by clarity of thought and much better decisions! It helps me every time.

Are you not sure where to begin? Do you need a push to get yourself moving?

You can make use of my short **self-questionnaire**, to create a breakthrough in your own thinking. This is a list of questions that takes you through the "who, what, where, when, and why" of your issue, and will help you find your own way to a new path around whatever referral obstacle you're facing.

My experience is that, in many cases, we already have the answers to the most important questions we face. We just need to gain clarity and perspective, so we can feel secure enough in our own instincts and ideas to take action on them.

FOR A FREE COPY of this self-questionnaire, email me at Referrals@JeffreyScott.biz — and put the words "self-questionnaire" in the subject line.

Ⓥ

THIRD-PARTY REFERRALS

Generating Referrals through
Professional and Trade Sources

What's the difference between a customer referral and a *third-party* referral?

Third-party referrals can be stronger.

FOR EXAMPLE: If you ask your attorney or tax advisor for the names of people who would benefit from working with you … and you then receive names and phone numbers … the quality of the referrals you receive is likely to be very good. After all, these people are paid to give trustworthy advice, and, presumably, they want to keep you as a customer.

When professionals give a client a reference, it is the same as giving professional advice.

YOU EARNED IT: You have a right to ask any vendor for a referral. Don't worry about whether you are the vendor's biggest customer or longest standing customer. Simply by virtue of paying these people, you have earned the right to ask for referrals.

Your chances for referrals will improve when you take the initiative to involve your vendors personally in your work. Don't just drop names or show them brochures; take them on a tour of a property you're particularly proud of and let them see for themselves. Let them experience your work first hand, and they will become confident in your work and they will refer you more eagerly.

Ask them, show them, involve them — and you will obtain more referrals.

Which vendors will provide me good referrals?

The list is a long one. It includes:

- **SUPPLIERS** who are also working on a job with you — which means, in essence, every allied professional with whom you do business.

- **TRADESPEOPLE** with whom you work side-by-side, such as builders and painters. Introduce yourself and strike up a purposeful conversation. Make sure you politely show them and let them experience the high quality of your work.

- **SUBCONTRACTORS.** This includes fence and tree companies, stonemasons, and the like — especially those you bring in on a job. After you bring them work, ask for referrals in return.

- **NURSERYMEN AND WOMEN.** These are people who work at, manage, or own, nurseries and garden supply outlets. They are a particularly rich source of referrals and networking opportunities. One landscape professional for whom I consult now gives design classes at his local nursery where he also buys plants. He has become known as the "go-to guy" at this nursery, and the employees their recommend him. The landscape professionals I know—through my speaking, consulting and The Leaders Edge peer program—have set up numerous networking opportunities like this to create referrals. It is not impossible to do, even in a down market. Someone is spending money, you just have to be creative and you can get in front of them.

- **STORES.** There's a flower shop with which one of my clients has a great complementary relationship. They send each other clients; it's a perfect arrangement. They don't compete with each other in any way, and they target precisely the same market.

- **PROFESSIONALS,** such as lawyers, retailers, and architects; opportunities to connect with these people are everywhere. So how do you start? Offer to take them to lunch, make a presentation at their office, or do both. It never hurts to ask. When you ask, the person will either respond with "Yes" to the date and time you propose, "Yes but later," (in which case you'll propose another date and time), or "Not now." Find out which it is!

You can cultivate referrals from anyone, anywhere. Set your priorities, make a plan, and go get 'em!

How do I motivate a builder or architect to recommend me?

When in doubt, ask. (Then follow up!)

Remember Woody Allen's famous advice, "Eighty percent of success is showing up." In this case, showing up means being in the right place at the right time. Find ways to tactfully introduce the idea of their recommending you, and follow up with them. Find ways to be top-of-mind with them.

R - E - S - P - E - C - T : As Aretha Franklin reminds us, people want respect. You'll receive more referrals when you earn their respect. This means being on time, polite, reliable, and, of course, respectful. You will find it easiest to build respect when you do things like attending their association meetings, participating in events important to them, and advertising in their association books. This will demonstrate that you are committed to building up the relationship, and that you are running a professional operation.

LET THEM EXPERIENCE YOU. Your goal is to find a way for this group to experience the quality of your work directly.

I recently set up an event where I invited the top architects in town to lunch with a client of mine. Her goal was to create a captive audience and give the architects a sense of the unique ways she could add value to their properties. The event was formal, a bit fancy, and very impressive. We had time to talk to them about her projects and abilities, and most importantly, we got to know the architects on a personal level.

KA-CHING! Help them earn money. Don't try to earn all of your money on your first job with them. Think in terms of the relationship, and remember that they need to make money too. Don't be so focused on the short term that you lose sight of who gave you the opportunity. If you are greedy, they're not going to invite you back.

FOR EXAMPLE: There was a situation when our company "owned" the client relationship and we invited in an architect to help us on a project. We eventually had to stop using the architect, because he got selfish and tried to subvert our relationship with the client — by taking over the budget for himself! Of course, we never asked him back. *Don't be the selfish partner in the relationship.*

MAKE THEM LOOK GOOD. Remember that, once you start working with professionals, you will more likely be asked back when you make them look good in the eyes of their client.

When you come right down to it, your job is to make other people look good for choosing you.

When someone does not know my work, how do I convince that person to refer me?

As a rule, professionals will only refer you when they know

1. You.

2. Your work.

3. Your reputation.

Ideally, the person should know about all three.

So when a specific property manager you're targeting doesn't know your work yet, she needs to know you. When she doesn't know you, she needs to know your reputation. All three avenues are important and worth pursuing.

Sometimes these efforts take years to pay off.

FOR EXAMPLE: I met an architect about eight years ago on a job. The job was cancelled; neither of us got any revenue from it, but I stayed in touch. He also put me on his personal mailing list. Every few years I got a birth announcement from him; when this happened, I would send a nice gift. Once a year, I called him; I probably e-mailed him once a year as well. Four years after we first met, I made a trip to his office; he gave me a tour and we discussed our businesses and how to help each other. Finally, last year, he sent my firm one job … and then another.

To date, he has sent us work in the low six figures … after eight years of staying on each other's radar screen!

Perseverance pays off. You need to have faith and continue on, when others would not.

Try to help the other person with their business, while politely impressing them with yours, and you will prosper.

GOLF, ANYONE? Inviting a professional or tradesperson to join you for a round of golf will get the person's attention and help create a personal relationship. Golf helps people get comfortable (or uncomfortable) with your character; at some point they will naturally start asking you about your work. If you are bad at golf, take lessons — or find out what sport the person you're targeting likes to watch — and then pass along an invitation to watch that sport. (Baseball tickets, anyone?) If the person doesn't like sports, invite him or her to lunch.

DOES ADVERTISING PAY? Sometimes it pays to advertise in the same city magazine where that person's firm advertises, especially when you're targeting a prominent company and prominent clients.

Our firm used to sell one large job a year from referrals we got from local builders we had never met. This happened in large part because of local advertising and marketing I was doing.

Advertising can be expensive, so use it only when you have a larger strategy in mind. Advertising is best when it supports a larger business-development effort, i.e. where you are purposefully trying to penetrate a specific area, with networking, direct mail and other kinds of marketing and public relations.

Consistent and effective advertising will build your reputation. Your audience will repeat and believe your advertising message, but only if you repeatedly advertise it yourself!

Be prepared to repeat your message regardless of the media you are using.

How do I create a *partnership* with another contractor to build referrals for both of us?

FIND A CONTRACTOR WHO'S A NATURAL REFERRAL PARTNER — someone who serves the same market you do, but offers a non-competitive, complementary service. Just for instance, find someone who offers plant health care if you maintain properties, or if you focus on hardscapes, find someone who focuses on softscapes. If you take down trees, find someone who installs trees.

Make sure your partner represents the same level of quality and integrity that you want to reflect in your business! When you partner with someone whose quality standards do not match your own, you will enter a nightmare situation that will harm your reputation and lose money. So follow the old human resources adage when it comes to finding this kind of partner: "Hire slow and fire quick."

We've developed a win-win business relationship with a local pond company. We use him as a pond consultant; he helps us with our property designs, and we use him as a subcontractor on our pond work. Moreover he refers maintenance clients to us.

This is a classic example of a win-win relationship that we have been nurturing for more than five years.

CREATE SERVICES: When you find a partner you trust, your next step is to create custom services that you can sell to his or her clients, or that the referring partner can sell to your clients. For instance, I know a contractor who maintains properties, and sells "plant health care" that he outsources to a trusted friend in town. They both make more money, and the client receives better service by working with just one main contractor.

CONTRACTOR SERVICES: You can also sell services aimed especially at-and-for the contractor — services that make it easy for you to stay in front of them and receive referrals from them. For instance: You might supply dumpsters or do excavation in support of the contractor's work. Or you might do "evaluation" work on their sites (tree evaluation, pool site evaluation, soil compaction analysis, or similar services).

Or you might do work on a contractor's personal home — perhaps at a discount if the contractor is willing to return the favor. This one doesn't always work; but sometimes it pays off.

FOR EXAMPLE: We perform swimming pool inspections for home inspectors and realtors who are helping their clients buy homes. Over the years, we have honed this service to a fine art, and we make it available to home inspectors at a good price. We market these services directly to this target market, which helps to keep us top-of-mind with them.

Even though the home inspectors are not supposed to recommend a contractor, they recommend us, because we are an "inspection" service just like they are and we go out of our way to help them, and make them look good. We have become their peers and they recommend us because we make their job so much easier.

Every year we do 10 to 20 inspections and make only "a few dollars," but a couple of these always turn into large maintenance or renovation jobs of the pool and property. Technically, the swimming pool inspection we offer is a small niche service, but it is a very successful component of our total marketing mix, and a source of good referrals.

What should I do *right now* to put the ideas in this section into action?

Visit "twelve in twelve." Write down the names of twelve professionals you should visit over the next twelve weeks. Pick a mix of contractors, professionals, people you already know, and a few whom you have not yet met, but want to meet.

SET THREE GOALS FOR EACH MEETING.

- What is your minimum goal? For example, finding some kind of personal connection with the other person—a hobby or person you both know.

- What is your main goal — the goal that will propel your business forward? For example, identifying a project where you can add value, or identifying an unmet need that you can fill for that person's clients.

- What is your bonus goal? For example, being invited to a high level party the other person is attending or hosting.

Develop these goals before you go to the meeting, so you can steer the conversation as the opportunity arises. Don't expect to make a sale at the actual meeting. Your goals for the meeting are not sales goals, but rather, next steps towards making a sale.

PRACTICE MAKES PERFECT. Put yourself in front of a number of quality people in order make a few quality connections … and build your networking muscles. Some people you meet will have opportunities for the coming year. Some people will like you and want to stay in contact, even though the opportunities they represent may take years to materialize. Some meetings will not amount to anything.

Learn when to move on, and when to stay in touch.

FREE ARTICLE: If you would like to learn more about how I dramatically grew my own referrals from realtors, e-mail me for a free copy my article "Harvesting Referrals from Realtors." My e-mail address is Referrals@JeffreyScott.biz. Put the words "realtor referrals" in the subject line.

Ⓥ𝐈

ALL TOGETHER NOW

How Your Employees Can
Create Referrals

How do I *structure* my business to maximize referrals?

The most powerful structure I know is: Create a one-on-one relationship between your client and a specific person in your company. This person may be you, or it may be someone with account management responsibility — someone who has the time and abilities to maintain a personal relationship. Ideally this person will become responsible for fulfilling your client's every (reasonable) need and wish.

MAKE IT PAY: How do you afford an account manager? By giving them enough services to sell their customers. In the process, they will be able to earn, and ask for, referrals.

Learning how to act like an account manager takes a change in mindset for some technically minded people. They may hate selling, but they love solving and preventing problems, and they usually love helping their customers maximize the joy of their property.

TEACH YOUR NEW ACCOUNT MANAGERS TO BE PROBLEM-PREVENTERS AND PROBLEM-SOLVERS.

NEW PRODUCTS: Develop new products and services to sell your customers. This will give your account managers more reasons to stay in touch with their customers. The more often you "touch" your customers, the more opportunities your account manager will have to generate sales … and referrals.

START SMALL: The client base you're targeting should have both the budget and the inclination to buy more, and if they do your job is to create more of the services they want.

Once you've decided to implement such a model, start small — with a single account manager — and prove that the product or service you're offering matches up with the buyers you're targeting. Work the bugs out before you expand your plan.

How do I teach employees across my organization to ask for referrals effectively?

FOCUS ON RELATIONSHIPS: You're not going to be able to train *everyone* in the company to ask effectively for referrals on a regular basis. All you can realistically expect of "all the employees" is that they do a *better job* of building relationships with their clients, which is the precursor to both asking for and earning referrals.

The challenge here is that different employees have different levels of relationship building skills. There is no magic wand you wave over your entire organization to make everyone excel at those skills. Therefore, each employee will need a different type and level of training.

DO WHAT WORKS: Start by teaching your people about the larger process of building relationships.

Show them what a successful professional relationship looks like. Does a team member already have a relationship with a favorite customer — someone with whom he or she has a good rapport? If so, how could your team member replicate that relationship with other clients?

Train on the job — by modeling the behaviors you want your team to make habitual.

Some people just need to see what good relationship-building skills look and sound like in action, so they can adapt the skills to their own style.

EMPOWERMENT: Before you release your employees and empower them to ask for referrals, check the basics. Do they know what it takes to complete the job per contract AND exceed the client's expectations? Do they understand the fine art of setting and managing expectations? Are they empowered to spend a few extra minutes to do the little extra things that you know will impress the customer? In my old company, we budgeted the extras. We budgeted the wow. Do you have a 'wow' budget?

Empower the members of your team to WOW your customers.
Show them how to turn that WOW response into a request for a referral.
Show them how to support the relationship over time.

How do I *motivate* my employees to generate referrals?

Start by helping them understand the connection between what they're good at and what actually results in referrals.

WORK FROM STRENGTH: Begin with *their* strengths, not yours.

- If they're technical people, show them how to build and support relationships using their technical skills.
- If they're designers, show them how to use their design skills to build and support relationships.
- Etc. (You get the picture.)

Working from their strengths will help them become more comfortable with the act of asking who else might benefit from a similar relationship.

Your job is help the members of your team become better at layering good communication skills on top of their existing technical skills.

REWARD YOUR TEAM for doing the right things up front — not just for the financial outcomes they generate. You want them to focus on doing the right things over time for your company's prospects and customers!

The rewards don't have to be financial. Money is not the ultimate motivator.

Most people are motivated by the prospect of receiving praise and recognition for doing a good job.

Although "Type A" personalities want to win, this is not an outcome that is always connected to money. You can reward many 'Type A' employees by playing to their egos rather than their wallets. But it's true that everyone needs their financial considerations taken care of, so make sure everyone is reasonably happy with that part of the equation.

For ideas on reward systems, see Section IX on incentives.

SHARING STORIES BUILDS UNDERSTANDING. Train your people by sharing "What Went Right" stories each week with your team. Have them share what they (or someone on the team) personally did to WOW a customer that week.

This approach does two things:

1. It recognizes the person who is engaged in the behavior you're trying to reproduce.
2. It passes good techniques along to the entire organization.

Consider this: The Ritz-Carlton hotel chain holds daily meetings like this — with 25,000 employees! What they can pull off in such a large, sprawling organization, you can surely pull off with your team of two, or two hundred people.

Can my employees become *too close* or *too personal* with prospects and customers?

Yes. That's why you must create and maintain policies and professional boundaries.

I once had an employee who got much too close and too personal with his customers. He spent his weekend time with his customers, went traveling overnight with them, and even started doing work for free. (Ouch!)

Not surprisingly, he also had difficulty collecting on unpaid bills. We let him go — even though he was generating quality referrals from his clients. I admit that I learned great techniques from him on how to generate referrals. I also learned the true meaning of "going too far." To be sure, there is a fine line between building a "personable" relationship and an "overly intimate" relationship, and you must notice when that line is being crossed.

LOOK FOR POSSIBLE WARNING SIGNS:

- Poor collections.
- Poor margins.
- Verbal contracts (such as unsigned change orders).
- Missed sales targets.

SET UP CLEAR GUIDELINES about taking gifts and other conflicts of interest.

Some companies have hard and fast rules, such as "employees cannot accept gifts over $50". Some rely on guidelines — like "Think of your team members first." Pick the approach that works best for your organization, and make it clear that you do have standards that must be followed. Remember, your best employees want your team to succeed; they want to

Can I expect *all* employees to network on behalf of my business?

Mostly yes — if you're willing to set the example and set realistic goals.

Begin with a core truth: Most employees will not network as well as the supervisor. However, the better the job you do — and the higher you raise the bar — the better the job the team will do. Be realistic and know that most will not hit your standard.

Expect incremental improvements.

Networkers fall into one of three categories.

1. BEGINNERS: Start by doing something simple with this group. Consider taking beginning networkers along to your industry association convention or similar events. Help your people become comfortable with the process of networking. Give them easy goals, like getting the business cards of three other people, and teach them how to engage in meaningful conversation. (By "meaningful", I mean "focused on and of interest to the other person.")

2. INTERMEDIATE: Those already comfortable with networking may choose to join associations of other industries, for example: BOMA (visit www.boma.org for more info) or your local home builders association. (For example, if you live in Atlanta, visit www.altantahomebuilders.com.) These are places where intermediate networkers will make friends with people who can refer business to your organization. Sometimes it pays (for you or employees) to become active at the committee or board level — this is often the key to becoming known and respected by the local "movers and shakers."

3. ADVANCED: The advanced networker should aim higher, joining business organizations, elite clubs or charities. This type of networking requires dedication, and will not generate productive contacts immediately. Anything worth having is worth spending time tending and growing. Plant the seed! The people who are already involved in these high-level organizations will want to see that you (or whoever joins) are committed and willing to help. That will take time.

It's not too much for your company to ask each and every employee to connect with one group, and donate time and build a network within that group, to the benefit of the company. Even if your front line staff donates just one day a year, that time investment will have a long-term impact.

FOR EXAMPLE: I know a landscape professional in the Midwest who asks everyone in his company to volunteer one day a year, on their own time, to a worthy cause. This is not mandatory, and not everyone in his company does it—but most do. Almost all of his employees donate their time to a couple of special causes that the company has developed a relationship with over the years.

His company is now seen as the go-to "green industry" company for these charities. This firm has received many requests for proposals and contracts over the years, in large part, because of its willingness to help these charities out. This example may not sound like "networking" – but when I heard that most every front-line laborer is actively involved and helping build the company's network, I couldn't help but smile.

This specific strategy will work for any company, of any size: The more employees you have, the more networking your company will do

How do *production laborers* create referrals?

Even if your production people don't have direct contact with clients, and even if they do not speak English, they can help generate referrals.

Remember that every point and position in which your organization "touches" your customer, you have the opportunity to impress your client and plant a seed for a future referral. We will look at just one example in this chapter — an example that is often under appreciated for it's importance in creating referrals.

POLISH AND PERFORMANCE: You will increase the chances that your fleet will generate a referral by training your drivers to behave in a well polished manner. This includes:

- Driving safely and courteously.
- Giving other drivers the right of way.
- Making eye contact, smiling and waving to other drivers.

I know for a fact that this works, because my company received calls all the time complimenting us on our inordinately courteous drivers.

> It is astonishing how the basic rules of kindergarten will help any company stand out above the competition. Be courteous and respectful of others.

BRANDING AT THE SPEED OF TRAFFIC: Your name, logo, website and/or phone number should be visible and legible from someone driving past you at 25 miles per hour. Keep this in mind, as you design your truck branding.

How do my front-line *office staff* create referrals?

We live in a "hustle-bustle" world — one in which everyone has too much to do. Use that fact to your advantage!

HUG YOUR CUSTOMERS: Train your office staff to make your company a place prospects and customers love calling! Give them a hug over the phone.

You probably already know whether or not this is happening. If customers routinely say, "I love talking with your staff on the phone!" — then it's happening. If you aren't hearing this, then you still have work to do. Start with the basics.

OUTSTANDING PHONE ETIQUETTE:

- Slow yourself down, take a breath, and answer slowly.

- Use a singsong in your voice and avoid monotone!

- Welcome your customer over the phone. When you find out who is calling, respond with, "I'm so glad you called, Mr. Smith." Make sure you repeat the customer's name. I guarantee this will make a difference in your caller's day!

One contractor I work with answers each incoming call with this phrase: *"What can we do to make this a great day for you?"* This often elicits a chuckle, and then a serious response from a first-time caller. I personally love this tactic because the customer remembers the unique phone call, and the conversation is automatically geared to the customer's wants and needs.

TREAT THE CUSTOMER LIKE A BEST FRIEND: To increase your chances of referrals, make a habit of returning calls as though it were your best friend calling. Too often, we are caught up in internal issues, and sometimes we treat callers more like interruptions than as best friends. When you treat customers well, they will be delighted to return the favor — by talking up their experience and sending you referrals.

For many clients, the quality of your phone contact is a clear indicator to your prospects of what they can expect from your company as a whole.

What if my staff has trouble generating referrals, *even after intensive training?* What do I do?

Take a closer look at your staff assignments. The problem may not be your training, but it may be the personality types of your staff.

TASK VS. RELATIONSHIP: You may have inherently "task-oriented" staff in charge of your customer relationships. If so, this may be one of the reasons the relationships aren't blossoming into referrals. You may need more staff who are inherently "relationship-oriented", rather than "task-oriented."

What do you do?

- Analyze your training efforts and frequency.
- Give your staff better systems for when they do come in contact with the customer.
- Review your bonus systems; it may have people pointed away from customer service and customer relationships.
- Hire an outside trainer or sales consultant to help.
- Perhaps most importantly, hire or promote relationship oriented people to take on account executive responsibilities.

REALITY CHECK: If your company *culture* is very task-oriented, then hiring a new person who is relationship-oriented could backfire. He or she may have trouble fitting in. Don't throw the person to the wolves! Work closely with him or her, to make sure he or she understands your culture and is accepted by your employees.

What should I do *right now* to put the ideas in this section into action?

CREATE A MODEL: Which one of your employees has the best networking results in your company?

- How does this person "meet and greet"?
- What does this person do to create relationships?
- How does this person follow up?
- How does this person follow the Golden Rule?
- What 'self-questions' and goals does this person use for guiding interactions?
- How does this person use e-mail? Snail-mail? Phone contact? Personal visits?

The answers to these questions point to a model that can be systematized and taught.

TO ANALYZE YOUR RELATIONSHIP-BUILDING EFFORTS, order a free a copy of my article "10 Rules to Rich Relationships" send your request to Referrals@JeffreyScott.biz and put "Rich Relationships" in the subject line. You will receive a copy of the rules my firm used to grow our business.

MAKE USE OF FREE HELP: How do you take this a step further? Write down your plan, and share it with someone. Get feedback from someone you respect in another industry, or from someone running a successful business similar to yours.

If you are not sure where to turn for honest yet productive feedback, consider joining a peer group to get help on this issue. This is one of the big reasons I started **THE LEADERS EDGE** peer program: to give contractors a place to get feedback and improve their plans, in a safe and productive environment. For more information, visit www.JeffreyScott.biz.

NETWORKING GROUPS
How to Use Them Effectively

A *paid* networking group is inviting me to join up — is this worth the money?

THE ANSWER IS YES —

- If you know that the people you'll be networking with are able to hire you directly, or able to directly influence others to hire you.
- If this is a group that you know for sure will open up access to the "movers and shakers" in your market.

THE ANSWER IS NO —

- If the membership is out of touch with your ideal prospect base.
- If you're selling a custom service, while everyone else in the group is selling a commodity offering. Or vice versa.
- If the group consists of business people who won't raise your game. (After all, the best reason to join a group is to improve yourself!)
- If the group is focused outside your geographic area.

BEFORE YOU COMMIT, ask to sit in on a couple of meetings. See whether you're receiving more YES signals than NO signals. Test the waters. When the group is not sufficiently high quality, move on, and test out another group!

I once joined a weekly networking group — BNI. In this particular group, I found that my type of services did not match up well with the type of services offered by other members in the group. There wasn't a good match, and I didn't get any qualified referrals. I am sure BNI works well for some — it just didn't work for my product in my market. So I left after three meetings. Experiment for yourself and use your own best judgement.

NETWORKING HAPPENS EVERY DAY: You don't need a networking group in order to network. You can work the process of networking wherever you go. Every morning, before you begin work, think about where you are going and whom you will meet that day. Think about what your networking goals should be for those meetings.

What's a good *alternative* to paid networking groups?

PROFESSIONAL ASSOCIATIONS make good networking groups, when you go to their events with the right GOALS in mind. Realistic goals include:

- Make friends and collect business cards.
- Leave a positive impression by demonstrating your character.
- Learn how others developed their businesses.
- Identify companies for potential collaboration.

COMMUNITY ORGANIZATIONS — such as the local chambers of commerce — can make for good referral opportunities … if you can gain synergy by joining. What is **SYNERGY?** Basically, it's killing two birds with one stone. For instance, one of my clients wanted to join a local business club, and he chose a club in a town which he knew had the potential to bring him a lot of business in the future. This was a double win for him: learning how to network within a club, and learning more about a new key town for him. When you join a group, be strategic.

CHARITIES are *sometimes* a good alternative, but pick them carefully or you will waste your time. Charities by their nature want you to give and give and give, so be cautious. Pick a group where your clients are involved, or where the most relevant movers and shakers are involved. Or pick a charity in your most important town. If you combine two or more of these criteria, your efforts will be more likely to pay off—but only if you are passionate about the charity's cause!

A contractor in my area uses his office as the drop-off point for the local "Toys for Tots" campaign each holiday season. People are constantly coming to his office, and he has built up a favorable reputation in town, and has grown his business. That's making double use of his facilities—that's synergy.

CREATE YOUR OWN: When the ideas above do not work for you, start your own networking group. Invite five people for a drink. Include various professionals, tradespeople, and possibly a potential client. Tell each invitee you have a couple of colleagues you want them to meet — people who will help them grow their business. Pick a quiet watering hole where you can corral the group. When people show up, your job is simple — buy each of them a drink, and introduce them to each other. (Thank you, Sasha ZeBryk, for this great idea.)

51

Where do I find the *best* places to network?

The secret is … ASK!

ASK YOUR BEST CLIENTS where you should join to find more people like them. If you're lucky, they may invite you to their favorite organization. When they do, and when the group has the kind of people you know for sure that you want to connect with, consider joining. Don't join because you feel you must; only join when you want to make a long-term commitment.

ASK THE GRANDDADDY COMPANIES. These are competitors in your area that are so secure in their leading position, that they don't mind helping you. Ask them, "If you were starting all over again, what organizations would you join? What organizations would you avoid?" They may even be willing to give you introductions that point you toward their favorite networking circles. You never know until you ask!

ASK YOUR BANKER. Here's an opportunity too many people overlook. Your banker is, by the nature of his position, well connected. Take advantage of that fact. My banker is a member of the State Legislature and has been in business for 30 years. When I need to know what is going on, or get help in the community, I simply invite him for coffee.

ASK YOUR BIGGEST VENDORS. Anyone you pay money to is going to be predisposed to help you. Make it clear to them you're asking for their help.

I find that some of my best networking opportunities come from a local magazine where I advertise. They throw good parties, and they are always careful to introduce me around when I go to their events. Ten years ago, I went to an event and met a wine cellar builder. We hit it off, and he referred us to two of his clients over the next few years. We got two big jobs … all because I decided not to go home early that night but instead went out for a few hours and put on my marketing hat.

What do I do once I show up for a networking meeting?

SHOW UP EARLY. Meet the host. Chat with him or her and establish a bond before other people show up. Make sure you have plenty of business cards on hand. Make a habit of offering your business card first; others will reciprocate.

USE CONVERSATION STARTERS. Memorize and use a few "failsafe" questions that work in any social situation, and then be an attentive listener.

- **"Do you have family?"** This is a great open-ended question; everyone has family, yet it allows the person to speak about the part of the family he or she wants to. It's safer — and easier — than asking people if they are married or have kids.

- **"Where are you from originally?"** This lets the person reminisce — and share happy stories from the past. Again, this question lets the person you've just met control the content.

- **"What did you want to be when you grew up?"** This usually makes people chuckle and it will often encourage them to tell you something interesting about their past. If they decide to answer this, and they usually do, they will open up to you in a way that normally wouldn't happen.

(Thanks to Boaz Rauchwerger for these great questions.)

ASK BUSINESS QUESTIONS. In a business situation, be ready to ask people what kinds of leads they are looking for in their business. Then offer to help them find a lead within your network. They will inevitably return the question. Of course, you must then be prepared with an answer about your own ideal client. Enjoy! This is the Rule of Reciprocity in action!

PIN YOURSELF. Consultant Ellen Ely recommends that you wear a pin on your jacket or shirt at these events. Perhaps you have a Rotary Club pin or a college pin or an association pin. A pin gives others something to speak about. For example: "What's the pin for?" Or: "Hey, I'm a member, too."

Initiating conversations is all about establishing commonality and rapport. That's what all these ideas are designed to help you do.

How will my *elevator speech* help me generate referrals at these events?

An elevator speech is a short story — sometimes just a few words — about you and your firm.

Your elevator speech should grab people's attention, and help them envision a perfect client for you. Have two elevator speeches ready for use at networking events: a three-second version and a ten-second version.

1. THREE-SECOND VERSION: This version should capture people's imagination and encourage them to ask more questions about what you do. When I was a contractor, I would say: *"I'm in the instant gratification business."* Or: "I make dreams come true." These answers always got people to SMILE and ask for elaboration. The beauty of this approach was that people were really listening to what I had to say. They wanted to know how I did what I did!

As a consultant, I now say, *"I help landscape professionals grow their company, build their wealth, and have more fun doing it."* People will usually raise their eyebrows, say "Really?" — and ask me how I do that.

2. TEN-SECOND VERSION: This longer version should focus on the benefits you deliver and the target clients you serve.

AS A LANDSCAPER, my ten-second version of the "elevator speech" went like this: "I help busy homeowners of multi-million dollar estates create and maintain the property of their dreams. I do this by providing a turnkey process with a single point of contact for the homeowner, so with the placement of a single phone call everything is taken care of; and when they come home, all they have to do is … enjoy."

How will my business card help me earn business at networking events?

To help you, your business card must be similar to your three-second elevator speech. It must attract people's attention, and make them want to take a closer look and ask more questions. Here are some ideas on how to pull that off:

Break the rules—make it different!

Take a look at all those boring me-too business cards out there—and break the rules!

OFF CENTER: Don't use centered text with boring type on your card. When all the words are centered, people's eyes just gloss over the card without reading it. Instead, create visual tension by having your card look "off center" in an aesthetically pleasing way. The front of my card is an extreme example that works.

Jeffrey Scott
President
Landscape Success Systems

tel: 203.220.8931
email: jeff@jeffreyscott.biz
web: www.jeffreyscott.biz
fax: 203.413.5583

Front

GIFT CARD: Turn your card into a gift certificate of some kind. It might say:

- Present this card for a free lawn evaluation.
- Go to www.blahblahblah.bla to download our free report: The 10 Most Common Mistakes People Make When Hiring a Lawn Care Company.

COLOR: Use color to capture attention. For example: If your company colors are red and white, use a white background with red type on one side, and a red background with white type on the other side.

SIZE: My card is slightly bigger than the normal business card size. So it sticks out slightly in a pile of cards. I have also seen cards with one or two smooth corners. Both of these ideas create a subtle difference that makes people pay attention to what you have handed them.

I often receive nice comments about my card. I hired a professional to design it, and the colors really pop! I hear many compliments, which means it makes a positive emotional impression, as opposed to just conveying data. This means people are more likely to remember me when I follow up with them.

Spend the money on good design!

But don't expect your business card to get you business all on its own — you still have to follow through and do the hard work.

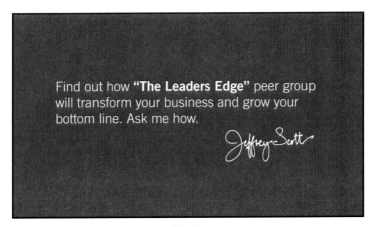

Back

What should I do *right now* to put the ideas in this section into action?

CREATE A NETWORKING EVENT:

Keep it simple. Here are some ways to start slow:

- Invite two people out for a drink; an existing client and a potential client. Call it a simple drink among friends—except these are two people who don't know each other, until you bring them together.

- If you have residential clients, invite two clients, and allow them to each bring along one of their own friends —someone new for you to meet!

- Or invite professionals; match up two professionals who would benefit from meeting each other. One should be someone who already works with you and can vouch for your work!

OR HAVE A BARBEQUE: If you are hesitant about doing this formally, then invite people to your home for a barbecue or a party. In that situation, you should invite between five and fifteen people. Invite a GOOD MIX of: prospects, friends, and people already using you and referring you – and thus willing to vouch for you.

Personally, I think parties work well. I have had a lot of fun over the years inviting people to parties whom I wanted to help. I never ask for anything in return. I make it about them, and I help them grow their business. One time I had a vendor over; I got up in the middle of the party and gave an impassioned testimonial for this person's service and dedication and knowledge. I shared stories about how he returned a call once from his vacation to help me deal with an emergency. I didn't ask him for a referral; I just focused on helping him grow his business—and you can bet he has returned the favor.

AUTOMATIC REFERRALS

How to Attract Referrals
without Asking for Them

What *single factor* is most likely to trigger an automatic referral?

YOU — going above and beyond the call of duty.

Follow the Rule of Reciprocity. You'll make a better impact when you give something than when you ask for a favor.

Give your clients a reason to do you a fovor!

"It is the characteristic of the magnanimous man to ask no favor but to be ready to do kindness to others." — Aristotle

In other words, be magnanimous and business will flow your way.

AN EXAMPLE OF BEING MAGNANIMOUS: Not long ago, we got a call from a businessman from India who wanted to build a swimming pool on his property. The appointment was quite awkward; we showed up with a man-and-woman sales team, and we quickly realized that in his culture women play a different role than we were used to in our culture. Yet something happened during that meeting that made all the difference in our prospect's mind. The appointment began early in the morning, before this prospect went to work. It was early winter and we just had experienced snowfall heavy enough to make driving difficult. At some point in the middle of this awkward appointment, he complained that his snowplow company wasn't showing up. Sensing an opportunity, we made a cell phone call to our company, and within a half hour we were plowing his driveway and shoveling his walks — at no charge to him. This made a lasting impression on him, despite the cultural differences. We eventually closed the sale. Here's the interesting part: that sale has grown into the single largest account ever at our company! We went from experiencing a profound "culture gap" … to our biggest customer ever, all because we helped someone out of a jam without expecting anything in return!

What is your *favorite strategy* for stimulating automatic referrals?

Treat your clients like more than *just clients.*

You will create an environment for automatic referrals when you connect with people at a level beyond the typical salesperson-customer. To do this, you need to connect at a person-to-person level, ideally in an environment outside of where you typically conduct business.

Here is a story from a green industry professional that makes the point.

"Jeffrey, after one of our monthly talks, I reviewed my client list for people who could help us achieve more sales. I picked my most important client, and made it my goal to get in front of him on a consistent basis. It started off with a phone call to check on his satisfaction, then a lunch invite. During this time, I made one rule for myself, and that was "don't ask for more work." I already had his business, so I did not want it to seem as though that was the extent of my interest in meeting with him. I kept in front of him with a couple more meetings for lunch; I even took him and his son to a Philadelphia Eagles game! During our meetings, I noticed that our conversations usually came back to business. He gave me ideas for add-on services and improving customer service, and the meetings always ended with his asking how I thought we could improve his property.

"Then, one day, I received a call from his family's construction business asking us to consult on a project at a new development of his. Next we received a call from a project manager who worked for his company, asking us to design a landscape for a high-end remodel project of his.

"The client that I promised myself I would never ask for business is now responsible for over $150,000 worth of work — from him, his businesses, and from referrals that he has sent our way. All it took was a true willingness to get on a different level with the client. I learned a valuable lesson from this experience: rather than just being a contractor to our clients, be a friend and advisor. I found that people really do want to spend money and help me succeed. I simply have to invest more than the time it takes to pick up their check."

How do I use *public relations* to generate automatic referrals for my business?

By avoiding the temptation to use public relations (P.R.) to focus on your own company and simply tout yourself.

The first rule of marketing: Focus on your customers and their interests, not on your own.

Try to avoid the typical self-congratulatory press release that describes your company's history, mission, or recent expansion. While there is a place for that kind of promotion, there are better ways to generate referrals.

Public relations is meant to raise your profile. There are two major ways to do this.

1. Find a pre-existing high-profile cause, and then support it in a way that will create a "buzz" in the community.

2. Create your own event.

EXAMPLE OF A PRE-EXISTING EVENT: An employee of ours was a competition rower, and her rowing club had a fundraising event. The event was going to be attended by many of the "movers and shakers" in our community. So we volunteered to dress up the entrance to the event; we made it look absolutely magnificent. We attended the event, and we made contacts with the right people; one of them called us the very next week for work. PR doesn't always work this quickly; the reason the response was so quick in this case was that our employee was a long-term member of the club. This was not a one-off attempt at exposure; rather, it was part of a long-term commitment to the club.

EXAMPLE OF A SELF-CREATED EVENT: SOUTHLAND LANDSCAPE MANAGEMENT, based in Charleston, South Carolina, created its own event by collecting clothes for the victims of a major flood in the Midwest. They invited other (competing) landscape companies to be involved, and they reached out to their community and asked for help; their employees were also happy to help out. As part of that larger effort, they reached out to the press and received great exposure.

It was a major P.R. coup, one that made them look like heroes. In fact, they are heroes for investing so much energy helping people in trouble, and for stepping up as selfless leaders in their community.

GARDEN TOURS: Consider working with your customers to put their properties on local garden tours, or feature their properties as part of a garden club event. These tours often attract hundreds of people (potential customers!) who are interested in gardens and garden architecture.

There are four keys to making this work:

1. Spend some of your own money primping the property so it looks picture perfect.

2. Staff the event with a sufficient number of your employees, so you can connect with as many attendees as possible.

3. Make sure your property experience stands out in people's minds. Do this by handing out drinks, custom pamphlets, gifts, and so on.

   At one event, our client served her grandmother's recipe for iced tea, and handed out the recipe during the event. This was not only very tasty...but also very memorable!.

4. Invite your clients to attend, and ask them to bring their friends along.

Any event that gives you the opportunity to mix with current and potential clients in a memorable and relevant setting will create automatic referrals for your business.

How do I get the *neighbors* of our customers to call us spontaneously?

Follow the basics.

LOOK THE PART: First and foremost, look and act professional at all times.

- Wear a uniform that conveys professionalism and makes a unique impression.
- A professional uniform is color coordinated: cap, shirt, pants.
- When possible, its accent (or main) color should be something other than green — in order to stand out from the competition and be easily recognizable by the neighbors.

*G*RASS HOPPER LAWNS from Larksville, PA does a great job of this. Their T-shirts are bright orange, with a blue-and-green grasshopper logo. Their uniform brings a smile to my face. I have seen many uniforms, and theirs is the best combination of creativity, attention-getting and professionalism.

...FROM A HUNDRED PACES. A good uniform should visually match with your vehicles and should be recognizable from a hundred paces away.

Why? Consider the following.

I was visiting with a client on my ritual visit of "How did the job go", which I made at the end of many of our big projects. The homeowner was telling me the story of how she chose us and how everything had gone. At that moment, one of our maintenance guys had driven up and was exiting his vehicle and walking towards us. She remarked that she loved the "detail" of our uniform – and loved the way it matched the "detail" of our work. For her, the uniform apparently reinforced our image of quality.

She then added that it was comforting for her, as a stay-at-home mom, to be able to recognize us coming from the top of the hill of her driveway.

She said that everything on our trucks and uniforms matched so well and she always felt good being able to recognize us from far away!

ACT THE PART: Most of the rules for "acting the part" equate to good old-fashioned common sense.

- No meals or siestas in public view.
- No shirts off when it's hot out.
- No loud music.
- No spraying the neighbor's vehicles when you're mowing and blowing.
- Don't ignore the neighbors, but smile at them; greet them in an upbeat way. Each time you enter and leave the job, make a connection!

REACH OUT: I like my company to call on the neighbors of each job we do so we can introduce ourselves and let people know that we are looking out for the safety of the neighborhood. Give people your card, and perhaps a brochure, and let them know how to contact you if they have any questions. When the job is over, check in again to thank them. If you caused a hassle, bring the neighbors some flowers and apologize for the inconvenience.

Referrals, like sports games, are won with perfect practice and solid execution.

How do I *follow up* with those who give me automatic referrals?

Give them a personalized "THANK YOU" message!

Do this in person, on the phone, or via a handwritten note.

If you don't have time for a visit and you can't seem to connect by phone, a handwritten note will stand out powerfully.

BUT...Don't send e-mail thank-you notes. They are too likely to be ignored.

In some cases, it may make sense to send a personal gift, such as homemade cookies, a bottle of wine, or gift certificate for the referrer and his or her spouse. If you're feeling particularly brave, offer to take both the referring person and the referral out to lunch or dinner together.

ESCALATE THE RELATIONSHIP: Once your relationship has reached the point where you are earning referrals from someone, look for ways to escalate the relationship. This is as simple as a shift from phone contact to face contact. Or a shift from an "all business" relationship to one that is more personal in nature.

FOR EXAMPLE: A landscape professional I know takes his best clients on a fishing trip with a chartered plane every year. (Yes, that's right. He takes his clients on a chartered vacation trip!) He spends some real money on this outing; in return, they spend real money with him! During this weekend trip these clients and my friend spend a lot of time with each other, talking about everything except business. As marketing ideas for our industry go, this has to be considered a radical idea, but it is nevertheless effective because it breaks down the barriers and escalates the relationship.

Take a chance — find a different way to say "Thank You."

Give people a reason to remember you and talk about you!

What does the person who gives me an unsolicited referral *expect* in return?

Most people simply want the CONTINUATION of the relationship, and RECOGNITION for the referral.

For most people, recognition simply means receiving your heartfelt thanks.

A few people will want something of substance in return; perhaps a discount on future services, or a commission.

Unless you have an arrangement for COMPENSATION ahead of time, you shouldn't be expected to take part in *quid pro quo*; but this is up to you.

See the section on Incentive Programs, to explore this subject further.

When you think a person may want something in return, the best thing to do is ask—with no premeditated assumptions. Ask if there is anything you can do in return for a referral. Ask a couple times—in case there is something that person wants but is embarrassed or hesitant to mention.

In my experience…

Most people want continued great service and some want a closer business relationship with you.

Someone gave me a referral, without my asking for it, but *I did not close the sale.* What do I do now?

Thank the person anyway.

You don't need to buy the person a T-bone steak, or give him or her tickets to the World Series….but an **"attitude of gratitude"** will go a long way toward supporting and building your relationship with this person. A thankful attitude will keep the door open for future referrals.

When your goal is to create a referral-based culture, it helps to:

Reward both the BEHAVOR and the RESULT.

This means thanking the person for the referral, no matter what comes of it; and thanking the person for the sale when the sale closes.

How you thank the person for a referral that has not turned into a sale yet is up to you. You might choose to express your thanks with a phone call, a note, or a modest gift.

Everything that happens to you is an opportunity.

This may sound cliché, but when you are served lemons, you can make lemonade. In this case, when you fail to make the sale, use this as an opportunity to reconnect with the referring person and reinforce the type of referral that best fits your business.

Anyone who wants to help you and is positioned to do so, is someone you want to spend time with and get to know better.

What should I do *right now* to put the ideas in this section into action?

Ask yourself: Where are my current referrals coming from?

Sit down and document all the ways you receive referrals.

DO A QUICK REFERRAL ANALYSIS:

1. What percentage of your new business would you estimate comes from referrals, i.e. from customer referrals, and from "other" referrals? What would you like the percentage in each category to be?

2. How good are you at setting and meeting client expectations?

3. Do you actively and constantly ask for feedback? How good is your feedback system?

4. How pleasant and exciting for your clients is your process, start to finish?

5. How many of your clients are wowed by what you do, and tell you so?

6. How much time do you spend with your customers?

Based on these answers, where do you need to improve?

The more you take this to heart, and the more client-centric you make your organization in each area of your company, including accounting, the more AUTOMATIC referrals you will receive.

FOR A MORE COMPREHENSIVE SELF-AUDIT, e-mail me and I will send you one written especially for the readers of this book.
E-mail Referrals@jeffreyscott.biz, and put "referral self-audit" in the subject line.

INCENTIVE SYSTEMS
What Works — What Doesn't

How do I know whether an *employee* incentive program is right for my company?

In my experience, most employee incentive systems have a limited shelf life.

They may capture your employees' interest and imagination up front, but after a while they lose their luster—either because your employees:

- Learn how to work the system.
- Become accustomed to the program and feel entitled to the extra bonus money.

The key is to change up the system after a couple years, or even after one year.

This keeps people on their toes and keeps things interesting. Tell your staff up front that your reward system is valid for, say, twelve months, and will be evaluated at year-end; and may not continue into the next year.

Here are elements of a good employee incentive system:

1. TEAM INCENTIVES: When you reward individual behavior you will naturally motivate people to look after their own self interests, and sometimes this creates more division than is good for your company.

Team incentives, on the other hand, are more likely to generate more company focus and impact, whether you are rewarding people for generating enhancement sales, creating referrals, or for making contributions in other areas where you want to see improvement. Team incentives typically reward values like sharing, open communication, peer support, creativity, self-management, and so on.

Individual incentives can lead to a lack of harmony, such as: not sharing, not communicating, not looking after ones peers, and not focusing on what is best for the company. In some situations, individual incentives will make sense, for instance, with territory salespeople.

No matter your system, remember that people "follow the money".

Take time to consider the behaviors you are likely to inspire with your reward system ... before you roll it out.

2. INVOLVE EVERYONE WHO WILL BE AFFECTED: Ask your people what they want as rewards before you implement the system. You may be surprised about what excites them. Often, your employees will want incentives that are different from and sometimes less costly than you are considering.

INVOLVE EVERYONE WHO WILL BE AFFECTED, AND YOUR PROGRAM WILL HAVE A BETTER CHANCE OF WORKING.

3. CONSTANT REVIEW AND FEEDBACK: All programs must be reviewed every year, if not more often. Look at the referral results, but don't only rely on the numbers alone. Ask the staff for feedback. Find out what worked well and what could be improved.

FOR EXAMPLE: A friend of mine who runs a large full-service landscape firm in Maryland told me how his company leased a skybox to watch the Redskins, among other things, as a reward for employees. The lease for the skybox was six years. For the first couple years the staff was very excited about using the skybox. But halfway through their lease, his staff no longer found the time or the interest to use it. This reward was great while it was still new and exciting, but after a while, it simply faded into the background. People had other business and family commitments that took priority.

OPEN BOOK: Some companies have opted to do away with employee bonus and commission systems altogether, and instead motivate their employees to the bottom line. Sometimes this is referred to as "open book management". I have heard of instances where this has worked well, and it replaces all the headaches and false starts of an ever-changing incentive system. If you want to learn more about this, you can google the term, or ask around at your national association meetings, or email me for more information.

How do I know whether a *client* incentive program is right for my company?

Consider implementing a formal incentive program for clients when:

- *You only see your clients rarely.* Perhaps you run a high transaction business, and your clients number in the high hundreds or thousands.

- *Your company sells a low-cost service.* In this case, an incentive would help the buyer get a large discount on their services relative to the price.

- *Your customers are looking for ways to save money.* If money is a main motivator for your clientele, then incentives can be helpful.

- *You have nothing to upsell and thus less reason to build a relationship.* If your product line is purposely very narrow, and you are not looking to sell your clients more services, then promoting an incentive system might be one of the reasons for you to get back in touch with them.

- *Incentive programs are the norm within your market niche.* If your clients expect this, and these systems work for your competitors, then you may want to experiment with this. If you are uncertain about this, ask around at your next association meeting.

- *No other contractor in your town uses client-incentive programs, and you want to stand out.* If you have asked around and found that no one is using incentive systems—this might be the perfect reason to experiment with one, as a way to give your company an edge when a customer is considering your firm.

Make sure any referral incentive program you select does not violate any professional ethics guidelines or local laws.

How do I choose the *right* client-incentive program for my company?

There is not a "silver bullet" that fits all situations.

Finding the right program takes experimentation, research, tweaking and periodic review. Here are a couple approaches that you may want to consider.

COMMERCIAL PROGRAMS: SOUTHLAND LANDSCAPE MANAGEMENT of Charleston, South Carolina gives out free flats of seasonal color, installed, in exchange for referrals from its commercial clients. The higher the referral contract, the more color they install.

In the words of the owner of Southland, "This referral campaign, although very simple, has done wonders in helping us cross sell within property management companies who are current customers — and it has helped us to sell to new prospects, as well! Since budgets are tight these days, adding free seasonal color, based on a referral and the execution of a signed contract, goes a long way. *In the last three months, we added $250,000 in new accounts using this program!"*

RESIDENTIAL PROGRAMS: One landscape company I know offers a month of free service for every referral that turns into a client. To qualify, the new clients must use their services for some minimum period, typically three months, before the bonus is paid. Such a system will be effective with a customer who knows your company well and loves your services. If you have long-term customers eager to earn free service by helping you out, this kind of arrangement is worth testing.

Client-incentive systems are not "one size fits all" solutions. You must experiment and find out what feels right for your company culture AND for the culture of your customer.

COUPON PROGRAMS: There is a place for coupons, if you are consistent in your approach, and especially if you sell a lower-cost service, where the discount makes a significant impact on the price.

SPRING-GREEN LAWN CARE, Plainfield, Illinois, has had great success with coupons. They reward their lawn care clients with Balloon Bucks that come in $10, $20 or $30 levels. The customer can refer a person to start the service and if that person starts, the referring customer receives $30, $20 or $10 off any service, depending on what was recommended. Referrals like this are an important element in the marketing plans of Spring-Green franchises.

Keep in mind, for a coupon to work, the customer still has to like you and the work you do. Coupons are not a replacement for mediocre service. People refer people they like and trust.

TWO-PART GIFT CARD: SPRING-GREEN also makes use of two-part gift card. One half is used as a thank you for using their service; it provides the customer a coupon for $30 off an additional service, such as core aeration or tree care. The second half is a referral card that the customer gives to a friend, neighbor or whomever – and if that person starts the service, that person will receive $30 off their lawn service.

This idea is **win-win** because the client feels good, and since "aeration" is put on automatic renewal, the franchise owner will make more money the following year. The key, according to Harold Enger of Spring-Green, is consistency. "The lawn care companies that have success with this system, are the ones that consistently make use of the coupons." Like any system, it only works when the people using it are following it consistently.

What *problems* should I watch out for when considering incentive programs?

The biggest problem is that the incentive program can work counter to the goal of growing your sales from existing customers.

If the incentive program takes your focus off the customer, you may be at risk of finding yourself with fewer enhancement sales and a drop in your "natural" flow of referrals.

When your goal is to increase ENHANCEMENT sales, be careful not to depend too heavily on client incentive programs. You still need to improve customer relationships in order to grow these sales.

Whenever I think about referral incentive programs, I am reminded of the so-called **loyalty programs** offered by the major airlines. I think many of these programs stand as a replacement for doing a great job and building a good relationship with the flying customer. That's not the kind of program I would want to set up.

Consider which kind of "airline" you want to become.

- Are you the "tired old airline," an organization that needs a complex loyalty program to make it logistically difficult for customers to switch to the competition?

- Or are you a "fresh new airline" like JetBlue, a company that provides huge value and that people love flying, with or without a loyalty program?

I have met very few people (if any) who are raving fans of the "tired old airlines" — in spite of all the loyalty programs they promote. Have you?

Should I consider paying *monetary* incentives for referrals?

Some companies use dollar-based customer incentives. This might mean giving clients, say, a $200 credit — once the referral they send your way does a minimum amount of business with you, perhaps $4000.

Using dollar-based systems will not work for everyone, because they point directly to money as the motivator.

Money as a motivator cuts two ways:

- Not everyone is motivated so directly by cash.
- Some people are too motivated by cash.

MY EXPERIENCE: Occasionally, realtors have asked me for financial rewards for bringing me clients. I've always said no. First and foremost, giving this kind of financial compensation is against the Connecticut Real Estate Laws & Regulations.

For me, this sort of incentive is problematic in another sense. A realtor who's on the lookout for a commission from me may not be looking out for the customer's best interests. At some point, there will be a conflict of interest between me, the client and the realtor—and this could come back to hurt the sale and my reputation.

For me, in this particular situation the risks outweigh the benefits. You, must make your own choice, based on:

- Your circumstances.
- The rules and regulations of your state.
- Your own company culture.

While monetary incentives do work, my overarching goal is to work with people who want to refer me because of my value, my standards and the quality of my work.

If I have no formal incentive program in place, should I reward customers *after the fact* for referring me?

Sure. It's the gesture that counts. And fortunately, most gestures don't cost a bundle.

It is the time and thought that you put into choosing a gift that counts.

One client who passed along a referral to us absolutely loved his luxury car. (He called it his "baby.") We picked up on that, and gave him a gift certificate for a free round of cleaning and detailing at an upscale car wash. He was ecstatic!

Another client who sent us referrals was a gardening and flower-show enthusiast. We gave her a very carefully selected flower basket. She loved it!

The cost of the gift: $35.
The emotion we elicited by customizing a thank-you gift for her: **PRICELESS!**

CREATE A STORY: If you don't know much about your client or if you don't have time to learn more about him or her, then yes, a nice restaurant gift certificate will do. But here's my challenge to you: Can you create an interesting story or theme behind this (potentially boring) idea, so as to create some excitement? Perhaps you could pick the newest restaurant with the most "buzz," or perhaps could you pick the very best restaurant in town, according to a local reviewer. Pass along a copy of the clipping, and you will let the person know that you chose the best restaurant for one of your favorite clients.

Create a MEMORY by creating a story to go along with your thank you gift. People remember stories!

Is it better to have the referrer *give me the name and number* of the referral, or simply pass my name and number on to the referral?

The right answer is: NEITHER.

It's best when the person who is referring you makes a personal introduction.

The next best answer is: BOTH.

When it is not possible to be introduced personaly, or when you run a high-volume business and don't have time for personal introductions, the next best option is to ask for the person's name and number … AND have your contact pass along your name and number.

CLOSE THE LOOP: When your relationship with the referrer is a strong one, take the following steps:

1. Ask your contact to reach out to his or her friend and have them ask for permission for you to call the friend.
2. Then ask your contact to call you back and let you know who was most interested in speaking with you.
3. Then call the referral.

This closes the loop on the process, and creates an expectation of your phone call.

MY EXPERIENCE: I once received a referral from a colleague of mine. He emailed me the name and website of a person he said I should call. I took him at face value, and contacted this person. It turns out the person was not expecting my call and he only vaguely remembered my colleague. As you might expect, the call didn't go as planned. I learned my lesson; it is always better to have your referrer give their referrals a "heads up" before you call.

WHOSE JOB IS IT, ANYWAY? Whatever path you follow here, there should be someone in your organization whose job is to follow up personally on referrals, regardless of who initiates the contact.

Should I use an incentive program with my *high-end* clientele?

Incentive programs pose problems for your most high-end clientele. I advise you take a different route with your high end clientele.

WHAT'S THEIR PERCEPTION? The problem is that offering to compensate a high-end client may make you look opportunistic and cheap. It is true that everyone, even your wealthy clients, loves a good deal. But your wealthiest clients don't want to be earning commissions off their friends when referring them. Rather, they are focused on finding someone to meet their higher-level needs.

HIGHER LEVEL NEEDS: Their needs are usually about something other than saving or earning a few dollars.

For the wealthy, time is more valuable than money.

They would rather *find and refer* someone who can save them time. They have the money to spend, and what they really want is for someone to make their life easier, and make their dreams come true. The pay off for them is huge: increased bragging rights and the simplification of their extremely busy life.

LOYALTY. High-end customers are very loyal. This saw cuts both ways. It is hard to convince a high-end client to switch; though once they have switched to you, and once you have proven yourself and earned their trust, they will support you even if you have a hiccup in your operations.

Earning their referral is straightforward. Focus your attention on servicing and even upselling these clients – rather than on trying to use incentive systems to motivate them to refer you.

How do I create a referral-incentive system that I can follow *when I am busy?*

Create an "ESCALATING" referral incentive system. Here's how:

DEVELOP A TRACKING SYSTEM to identify which clients are referring new customers.

IDENTIFY MULTIPLE REFERRAL TIERS, so that clients with more profitable referrals receive more upscale "THANK YOU" experiences.

RECOGNIZE "REPEAT REFERRERS" — customers who give you multiple high-quality referrals. If you are too busy in season, pre-prepare an assortment of bonus gifts while you are still in your "down time" period: gift certificates, plants, credits toward free work from your company, that kind of thing.

ASSIGN THE COST of the gifts to your marketing budget. Or build the cost of the referral gifts into the contract proposal for your new customer, so you never need to pay out of pocket for your referrals. The first idea may seem cheaper, but it may be just as cheap and in fact easier to create a referral marketing budget, that gets paid out of your overhead. It is up to you.

Here's an example of how it might work:

1. A client or friend leaves you a voice mail message giving you the name of a person who might be interested in working with you. Or, a lead calls you and mentions the name of the person who referred them.

2. Call that referring person back within one business day to say "thank you," and then, when possible, gather more information about the referral.

3. When the referral results in an opportunity to bid on a project, you write a personal THANK YOU note to the referrer. If the introduction was a very important one, you give them a more valuable thank you.

4. When a sale results in work for under $10,000, you deliver a unique gift basket to the referrer. You can find these online, and create an easy process to order them and have them delivered.

5. When a sale results between $10,000 and $75,000, you give the referrer a gift certificate for dinner or two bottles of very fine wine.

6. When a sale results in work over $75,000 but less than $150,000, offer the person a choice from a selection of high value gifts. Possibilities include: tickets to a pro game for guys, a case of good wine for couples, a day at a fancy spa for women. You get the idea. Let the person choose the best gift! Remember to set all this up ahead of time, so that in-season you are executing a well-oiled referral system.

7. For referrals over $150,000, you combine gifts, or, better yet, find out what the person really loves, and create a gift especially for them.

Your typical sales may on average be smaller, or they may be bigger. Come up with a system that reflects your typical sales size.

This system is called "escalating" because the larger the referral sale, the larger the gift you give. The key to a good referral system is to keep it easy to implement. So use the KISS approach: keep it super simple!

Moreover, handing out rewards should feel good for all parties involved. It is critical to make a BIG DEAL when handing out rewards. You can not simply drop it in the mail. You should present gifts in person, and if you do mail the gift, wrap it in such a way that the recipient will greatly enjoy the unwrapping of it. In other words, make it appear special.

The bigger deal you make, the more the recipient will appreciate it!

How do I know whether my incentive program is *cost-effective?*

You must first review your program on a stand-alone basis, and then compare it with your other marketing programs.

Sometimes a customer-referral incentive system will cost more per new customer than other forms of marketing. For example, it might be less expensive to use direct mail or pay a commission to a salesperson to generate their own referrals.

But is that reason enough to drop your incentive program?

ANALYZE THIS: Calculate the ROI (return on investment) of each program separately.

Then compare them.

USE THE FOLLOWING CASE STUDY: Assume that you use four programs:

> 1. Client-incentive system for referrals
>
> 2. Salesperson referral bonus
>
> 3. Yellow Pages advertising
>
> 4. Direct mail

Even if one program (for instance the yellow pages) earns a much lower ROI than your other programs, it might make sense to keep all four programs ... assuming you answer the following questions in the affirmative:

- Does each program earn you a minimum acceptable profit? (The definition of acceptable will depend on your business model and the aggressiveness of your growth plans.)
- Can you handle the new business from all of the programs?
- Are you also able to take advantage of all your internal upselling opportunities, while also handling all these outside leads?
- Do you have the infrastructure capacity to handle the growth? (By "infrastructure," I mean management, space, equipment, employees, subcontractor relationships, and so on).

- Are the leads from all these programs easy to close? Or does one type of lead require a lot more sales time to close?
- Are these the right leads for you? In other words, will they help you grow your business long-term in the direction you want?

If you can't answer all of these questions with a positive response, you should start considering cutting back programs that are low performing.

A good marketing program requires constant testing. Even though your program is working for you this year, you might decide next year to test out new ideas while simultaneously executing your "old reliable" program. The rule of thumb is, keep the old marketing tactic until you find something that directly replaces it and does a better job. If the new marketing tactic complements something that is already working for you, keep both programs.

Always be testing new marketing ideas,
but don't just throw away the old ideas.
Measure and compare results.

What should I do *right now* to put the ideas in this section into action?

IF YOU DON'T HAVE AN INCENTIVE PLAN IN PLACE – identify a place in your business where you can experiment with one.

But don't just roll out a program – test it out, and see if it catches on with some clients, before you formally make it official.

Start with a survey. If you have multiple client groups, start with the group that you think will be most open for this. Ask your clients if they would be motivated to refer you if you offered an incentive. Speak to five to ten clients and see if you get a strong hearty "Yes." If their response is lukewarm, then approach a different segment of your clients.

Once you roll out a plan, you can then set it up on your website and create marketing handouts for your staff and office to use.

IF YOU ALREADY have an incentive plan in place, then calculate the ROI of the plan compared to your other marketing programs. Do a formal review of your existing program; speak to your clients and employees and identify obstacles to its success.

For a copy of the chart I use to analyze ROI, email me at Referrals@jeffreyscott.biz, and put "Incentive ROI" in the subject line.

QUALIFYING
THE REFERRAL
How Good a Lead Is It?

Why should I *bother* to qualify referrals? Aren't they all good?

Not all referrals are created equal.

You can't assume every referral that calls you, or that you call, will be a qualified match for your business; hence, you need to qualify the referral leads you receive.

ONE OF THE BIGGEST MISTAKES people make in our industry is not qualifying their prospects over the phone before they invest time and resources to visit the prospect.

Why do companies avoid qualifying their prospects?

Sometimes they are afraid to make a mistake or to miss a sales opportunity. Or they feel guilty and believe that they have an obligation to meet with all prospects that call them. If you do this, you will end up giving bad prospects as much attention as you give good prospects. This will dilute your time, energy and your sales!

THE BEST OUTCOME happens when you allocate your time strategically between two groups:

- Your most promising prospects.
- Your current customers you wish to upsell.

The only way to do this is to prioritize your time and qualify your referrals more stringently.

THINK TWICE. You do not owe it to your referrer to meet in person with every one of his or her referrals … unless you promised to do so, or unless the person who gave you the referral happens to be incredibly important within your business network.

In all other situations, treat each lead with courtesy and respect — but treat yourself and your existing clients with MORE deference and respect, by prioritizing who you go to see in person.

What are the *best* ways to qualify a referral?

There are many processes for qualifying referral leads. Here is what I recommend:

1. **IDENTIFY THEIR PRIORITIES.** Find out what's most important to them and what they're trying to accomplish. What are they looking for from you, and does it fit well with your idea of your ideal client? The answers to these questions will tell if there is a good "fit" with your company.

2. **FIND OUT WHETHER THEY KNOW YOU.** Find out what they already know about you. The more they already know about you, the more likely they are to hire you.

3. **FIND OUT WHETHER THEY HAVE SEEN YOUR WORK IN PERSON.** If they have, and they like what they've seen, they are predisposed to work with you. However if they haven't seen your work before, it is not a deal-breaker.

4. **IDENTIFY THEIR TIMING.** Do they want it done tomorrow? Next month? Sometime this year? Or do they have no idea?
   As you pay attention to timing, you will see a pattern emerge.
   For my firm, the pattern is: "the longer their time frame, the more qualified they are". For your firm it could be the opposite.

5. **FIND OUT HOW THEY DESCRIBE THE WORK.** This means more than just figuring out what's on their to-do list. It means listening to the *language* people use to describe the outcomes they desire. Does it match with how your ideal clients speak?

6. **FIND OUT HOW MUCH CONTROL THEY WANT.** Are they looking to control every aspect of the job? Or are they looking for your leadership, and are they willing to follow the processes that your company uses?

The best high-end clients want leadership. While it is in their nature to want control, it is more important with them to get the very best in quality. High-end clients like working with experts.

7. IDENTIFY OUT HOW THEY SPEAK ABOUT MONEY AND COSTS.

    a. How educated are they about costs?

    b. How familiar are they with your cost structure?

    c. Are they complaining about the cost of the last contractor they hired (or fired)?

    d. Are they even willing to speak with you about money?

    e. What kinds of questions does the person ask you about pricing?

    f. What happens when you mention a price range for the kind of project this person is envisioning? A very broad range can effectively "force" a silent prospect to give you some kind of response about money; a very narrow range may help you disqualify someone whom you suspect will not be able to afford you.

8. LEARN WHY THEY'RE CALLING YOU. What is the *underlying reason* for the call?

    a. Did they fire their last contractor?

    b. Are they price shopping?

    c. Are they looking for leadership and want your help?

    d. Are they fishing for free ideas?

By the end of your conversation with them, the answers should become clear.

9. ASK HOW THEY HEARD OF YOU. It is important to always track the answer to this question, in order to steer the growth of your firm and ensure a HIGH *return on investment* in your marketing programs. The proper question to ask a new lead is:

"What made you pick up the phone and call us?"

If you have been in business a long time, some of your leads will tell you they have "just heard of you". Your job, when qualifying them, is to find out which element of your marketing motivated them, or caught their attention, when they finally decided to pick up the phone and call you. Track the answer to this question, in order to determine return on investment. If someone gives you two answers to this question, you should consider tracking both answers.

What should I do if the referral turns out to be a *bad* lead?

Your job is to make every lead feel good for calling you.

Remember: even though the lead may not be qualified, it still connects back to your base of clients, customers, and advocates. Treat all people you meet as someone who can further your reputation.

ON THE PHONE: If, while on the phone, you sense the referral lead is not a good one, switch to consultant mode. Consider sharing advice that will help the person accomplish their goals. Direct the person to an alternative service provider or to a resource guide that will be helpful in locating another service provider.

IN PERSON: If you have already invested travel time, and you find that this isn't a good client for you, find a way to let them down easy.

For instance: "I'm glad I had a chance to come and meet you since you are a friend of Mr. so-and-so, unfortunately this job is not our specialty."

Then go into consultant mode and attempt to help the person. Give him or her some questions to consider. If they are open to it, offer them a couple ideas that will help the person feel good about having called you. Again, if you feel comfortable, direct them to a service provider you already know and trust. What goes around, comes around.

IF THE REFERRAL WAS A STRONG ON: You will want to circle back and let your referrer know how you handled the lead.

No matter what happens with this lead, remember that someone who *doesn't* turn into a customer still has the possibility of referring you to someone who will!

Everyone is a potential source of referrals.

What should I do *right now* to put the ideas in this section into action?

The fastest way to make a positive impact on your sales is to implement an effective process for qualifying prospects. This helps you in two ways:

1. Eliminating time wasted traveling to meet with bad leads

2. Improving the closing ratio of good leads.

This process is called *"push-pull."*

A PUSH-PULL LEAD QUALIFYING PROCESS pushes away bad leads, while pulling good leads closer to you and increasing your statistical likelihood of closing them. Do the following to integrate a push-pull process into your company:

FIRST, measure where you are currently. How much do you sell per lead category? Divide this dollar figure by the number of appointments you go on, and this will tell you how "valuable" each lead category is. In other words, how much you sell on average per appointment.

To better understand this, email me for a spreadsheet that shows you how to calculate the value of each lead category. Send your request to referrals@jeffreyscott.biz, and put "measuring lead value" in the subject line.

SECOND, audit your qualifying process. Ask the following questions:

- Do you uncover enough information to understand your prospect's underlying motivation, needs and wants? Refer to the questions covered above in this section.

- Are there places where you could use more *soft and hard qualifiers?*

    Soft qualifiers give the prospect an emotional impression of your firm. For example, when your prospect comes in contact with a brochure or a process or a website that speaks to your quality level, he or she will start to make subconscious decisions about your firm.

Hard qualifiers force your prospects to make actual decisions; for example: we only take appointments on weekdays, or we charge a token fee for the first appointment, or the process we follow has you coming to our showroom for the first visit. These all require the prospect to make actual decisions.

If you are unsure about the seriousness of a lead, you can mention a price range over the phone in order to better qualify the lead's intentions.

- Do you use adequate marketing tools and customer service techniques to excite your prospect? Do your good prospects become progressively more excited about working with you, based on how you treat them and lead them through the decision making process? This is how good leads turn into great leads.

THIRD, find holes and implement improvements in your process, and track your new results compared to past results. You should see the value of your appointments going up — because you're going out on fewer total appointments, and closing more of the appointments you do go on!

MEASURE IT
Benchmarking and Tracking
Your Referrals

What *activities* should I be executing — and tracking — to ensure more high-quality referrals?

It is important to set targets for both activities and results. You may not get all the results you want initially. You need to track the right activities, along with the results, in order to build the habits that will deliver the results you want.

Measure the activity, not just the end result!

THE RIGHT ACTIVITIES INCLUDE:

- *Constantly reviewing quality.* In the landscape world, this means walking the property. Doing so helps control quality and builds customer relationships. You are likely to generate upsells with these walks, and you will also drive referrals by staying in front of the client. For some clients you will do this weekly, for some monthly, and some will require it less often.

- *Top 25 people.* Keep a list of the top 25 people who do or could refer business to you, and keep track of what you do to connect with them every month. Do you mail? Call? Write? Visit? Every employee responsible for business development should have his or her own list.

- *Total calls to action.* This is the number of times you give a client a new idea (or a proposal) to act on. It is important that you do this with your *consultant* hat on; you must be perceived as helping, not selling. Come up with new ideas once a month for those in the "maintaining" business, and weekly or daily for the "project-based" business. If you keep track of how often you suggest new ideas, you can hold yourself accountable to this new habit.

- *Total networking.* How many networking events do you attend? These can be events created by your company, or events held by someone else. Measure this quarterly, and measure the follow up. Your goal is to build up the list of prospects and influencers who can help you — and whom you can help.

- *Number of "inner circle" client relationships.* These are the clients with whom you have a close, special relationship. Those that may invite you for a drink or a meal; those that invite you into their inner circle of friends or associates. These are clients who buy work from you or refer you continuously. Keep a list of these people handy, and track what exactly you do with them every month or even every week. You may only have a couple of these relationships; if so, see what you can do to add "just one more" of these types of relationships to your black book. These are very special relationships that are nurtured one at a time.

- *Number of total "meaningful conversations" with customers.* This metric is helpful for those responsible for business development. There is a ratio of the number of "meaningful conversations" you need to have each week, in order to close one sale; it differs by company and industry. It is especially important to track if you are new to your job of business development.

DON'T BE OVERWHELMED. This list is just a starting point. If time is limited, just pick one place to improve. You also may come up with activities that you want to add to this list, and you may feel that there are items on it that don't apply to your business. Do what feels right for YOUR business!

Any tracking system is meaningless unless it connects to your company goals. Tracking identifies results, so track the things that are truly meaningful to moving your marketing, sales and business plans forward.

What *results* should I track, regarding the referrals that we actually receive?

You need to track a few simple things.

TRACK THE SOURCE, be it customers, architects, builders, nurseries, or any other group.

TRACK THE NAME, and use a system that connects the name to the larger group the person belongs to: Mr. Smith (the architect), Mrs. Fields (the client), and so forth. Among other things, tracking these names will remind you to thank and reward those who refer business to you.

TRACK THE NUMBER OF REFERRALS by year, on a monthly basis.

TRACK YOUR SALES BY SOURCE, so you know what percentage of your sales is coming from each of the referral sources you've identified.

TRACK THE VALUE OF EACH LEAD. This was discussed in the last chapter of the previous section. Review that chapter for how to calculate this number.

TRACK ALL OF THIS BY COMPANY DIVISION. You want to know which divisions are doing better than others, or worse than others, when it comes to referral generation.

TRACK WHICH SALESPERSON is getting referrals, and which one isn't. This will be important information for your incentive systems. Knowledge is power!

TRACK HOW MAY REFERRALS YOU GET PER CUSTOMER. Some companies look to get one referral (or more) per customer per year. This is not a target I recommend for most businesses, although it makes sense for some companies that are heavily oriented towards business development. I will share some advice for these companies in the next chapter.

The reason you are tracking this data is to answer questions like the following:

- Are your proactive business development activities working?
- Is anyone sending you repeat referrals?
- Are you getting significantly more referrals from a particular division?
- Is a particular division lacking in referrals?
- Are new referral sources popping up that you should be pursuing?
- Are you meeting your overall referral goals?
- How are you doing compared to last year when it comes to generating referrals?

USE THE CATEGORIES YOU SEE LISTED HERE AS A STARTING POINT.

Pick the measurements that best support your company's specific goals. It is important to be consistent, year after year, in tracking against those measurements.

Consistency is king when it comes to tracking and measuring!

Should I expect every customer to give me a referral each year?

There are two schools of thought here.

SCHOOL ONE maintains that, as long as enough business comes through the door, it doesn't matter where the referrals come from. What you care most about is the percentage of new business you derive from referrals.

AND WHAT IS THE RIGHT PERCENTAGE? Unfortunately, there's no simple answer that applies across the board. Some companies shoot for (and reach) the goal of getting 100% of their new business from referrals – but hitting that number may mean they're NOT growing their business as fast as they could be. Some companies are happy with 50% of new business coming from referrals. I personally like a goal around 80% +/-, for all the reasons discussed in Section I.

PURE MAINTENANCE companies can grow by means of referrals alone, assuming they are not looking to expand aggressively and they have a high client retention rate. But once you add other services to sell, it helps to have the synergy of marketing helping to drive your growth.

SCHOOL TWO holds that every account manager should get a few (one, two, or three) good referrals from each of his or her customers, every year. According to this school of thought, generating these referrals is one of the ways an account manager justifies drawing a paycheck. It's part of the job.

This is how insurance companies operate. They rarely get business from advertising or from "cold" leads. As a general rule, they get most of their business by means of a referral of some kind. Insurance agents typically aim to get referrals from each and every customer.

EACH MARKETPLACE IS DIFFERENT, each industry niche has a different tendency to be able to grow by referral, and each company has unique strategic objectives. You have to set a goal that makes sense for you.

What should I do *right now* to put the ideas in this section into action?

Track your TOP 25!

You can get started easily by identifying and tracking your top referrers—those that do refer you and those that could refer you.

START SMALL. You may not have 25 people to put on your list. You may only have five or ten at first. That's fine. Put the names on a spreadsheet and review the sheet monthly, making sure you do something once a month with each of these people.

If you don't have time to call each person monthly, you can do the following:

- Write a letter.
- Send a mailer .
- Do the person a favor, something that is "low-cost, high-value."

Set up a schedule. Make it easy to follow. Use the "Mail, Call, Visit" system. Remember that success in marketing and business development usually comes down to a few simple things done repeatedly.

THE SIMPLEST SYSTEM I ever heard of was from a salesperson who found a reason to send everyone on his list a card once a month. He sent a card on their birthday, on the anniversary of their first meeting, on the holidays, and even on his own birthday. This was a PERSONAL card that went out every month, like clockwork. It was all he used, and it worked extremely well to grow his business.

Show you care. Stay in touch. Have some fun with it.

MAY I HELP YOU GET STARTED?

If you want, I can send you a sample "calendar" that you can use to stay in touch with your top 25 referrers (and potential referrers). Simply e-mail me at Referrals@JeffreyScott.biz. Put "TOP 25" in the subject line.

BEATING
THE ODDS
Improving Your Chances of
Receiving Good Referrals

A customer has volunteered to help me get referrals. What do I do?

Start by giving her a supply of brochures and possibly business cards to hand out. The materials you pass along should tell a story, by showing people:

    a. What you do.

    b. How you're both different and better than anyone else at what you do.

    c. What overarching need you solve for your customers.

    d. How to get in touch with you and take the next step.

Then – keep in touch with your customer who has offered to help you. Since it was this person's idea to get referrals for you, it's perfectly appropriate to ask her from time to time whether she needs any more materials from you. Of course, checking in also serves as a tactful reminder of her promise to promote your firm.

WEDDING TOAST. A friend of mine experienced the benefit of this approach. The people who planned his wedding party asked him whether he would spread the word on what a good job they were doing. My friend said "Sure," and received a bunch of brochures to hand out. He handed them all out, and he brought in at least one new client to the party-planning firm. My friend was enjoying the party planning process so much that he was more than happy to tell all his friends about what a great job they were doing.

The process excited their clients, and the wedding planners made good use of that excitement!

How are you taking advantage of your clients' excitement?

We are new and don't have a huge client base – so how do we generate referrals?

New businesses that make it past the first year of operation tend to grow much more quickly than older, larger businesses. Why is this? For one thing, the person at the top is closer to his or her customers, and tends to give those customers better service and more personalized attention than the "big guys" do.

In other words, your small size is NOT A DISADVANTAGE. Rather, it is a BIG competitive advantage.

Small companies can grow more quickly than large ones.

FIND WAYS TO EXPLOIT YOUR SIZE. For instance:

1. Make your company's size one of your selling benefits. Tell your prospects how they will get more personalized attention — and then show them exactly what you mean during the sales and fulfillment process. Make a habit of this, and you will generate ample referrals.

2. Stay in touch with customers after the sale is made. The boss of a small firm can do this more easily than a larger competitor who has hundreds of clients. Taking advantage of that one fact alone will mean more referrals for your business!

3. As the owner of or manager in a fledgling business, ask your clients to help get the word out about your firm. Let them know your business plan, and your passion, and they will help you, assuming you are giving them 100% of what they need.

AMERICA IS THE LAND OF OPPORTUNITY. PEOPLE LOVE HELPING PEOPLE WHO HELP THEMSELVES!

Knock yourself out for your customers. Do right by them. Tell them your expansion plans for your business, and ask for their help in getting you there. You may be surprised at how helpful they will be.

Is there a particular personality type that is more likely to give a referral?

YES!

THE CONNECTORS: Certain clients are "connectors"—people who tend to have many friends or get involved in social causes. Either at home or at work, these people live to connect! Connectors will naturally refer you to others … *if* you give them a good reason to do so, and *if* you stay on their radar screen.

There's another group you should know about, too …

THE "QUIET" PEOPLE: Bear in mind that you also get referrals from people who seem quiet and reserved and DON'T appear to have lots and lots of friends. These people often have something in life that they are passionate about. Perhaps it's work, or a local charity, or a club in which they are long-time members. Very often, these folks have their own mini world where they spend their time – a world that's "miniature" compared to the world of connectors, at any rate. You want them handing out your name and contact information within that world! Good things will happen for you when they do.

FOR INSTANCE: I had a client who was very quiet and reserved. He definitely wasn't a classic, extroverted connector, but he certainly knew the "right" people (i.e. those with money.) This client worked at a high-powered financial company. He lived in an upscale town and had kids who went to elite schools. After he became our customer, we kept him very happy … so happy, in fact, that he began to take steps to help us grow our business, by getting us exposure in the right circles within his community.

THE MORAL TO THE STORY: Make it a priority to get close to the connectors… but don't forget that your other clients and contacts, including the silent types, have their own connections and reasons for referring you.

Is it too bold to ask clients to write a letter of reference?

Not at all. Many clients will be delighted to write you a letter of reference, and will be very happy that you asked.

The act of writing a letter of recommendation will help to remind your clients why they hired you and why they like doing business with you.

DON'T MISS YOUR CHANCE! When you hear a client compliment your work, feel free to ask, "Hey, do you mind if I put that into writing?" Or: "Hey, do you mind if I put that on my website?"

Perhaps you're wondering: Is it really okay to VOLUNTEER to write the letter of recommendation for the client?

ANSWER: Yes! This makes it easy on the client! Simply offer to send the client an e-mail message they can approve or edit as they see fit. You will be surprised at how often the client agrees to allow you to write the first draft of a recommendation letter. The better your relationship, the more leeway they will give you when it comes to creating the letter of recommendation. Create something that stresses your value to the client, and perhaps include a story of something you did that saved the day and/or WOWed the client. If you are unsure what to emphasize, provide two prewritten testimonials and let the client pick the one that seems best.

I have a very busy client, who doesn't get much time to sit down and write. He wanted to help me grow my business, and he was genuinely relieved (!) when I offered to send him an email with a sample testimonial. I sent him three and he picked the one that resonated with him.

Remember to get authorization to use these testimonials on your website.

What format should the final letter of recommendation take?

There are three main formats to consider when obtaining a letter of recommendation:

- **ON THE CLIENT'S LETTERHEAD.** This looks great if the client is a well-known individual or works for a recognizable company. Unfortunately, asking for the letter on the client's letterhead invariably slows down the process of actually getting the letter.

  Some clients will send you an unsolicited letter. I usually ask permission to take a blurb from their letter, and use that portion on my marketing.

- **BY E-MAIL.** It is much easier to get approval for a letter of recommendation by e-mail. If the person is serious about helping you out, the whole process can be done within a couple days, or a week at the most.

- **IN A ONE-PAGE DOCUMENT.** You can also create a document that features both text and a photograph of the work you did. This can be quite powerful. Try to get permission to use a picture of the client, too, so you can showcase the human-interest side of your work. Create a headline that states the main benefit of hiring you, and a subheading stating what you did. Then use the testimonial as the main body copy, describing the further benefits and positive emotions surrounding your work.

CAVEAT: Be careful not to put your customer's address or phone number on your website. Even if the client gives you permission, this poses an unnecessary security risk to them, and thus to you.

Can I assume my clients know that I need their referrals?

NO! Most of your clients are not aware that you need their referrals. Especially if you're running a larger company, your clients will tend to assume that you are busy and happy enough already, and that you don't need their referral.

This makes sense, right? Think about it from their perspective: You don't stay in touch like you used to, and you are sometimes late for appointments; and clearly you are always running around from appointment to appointment. By those external measures, you appear successful — and you no longer need them to advocate for your firm. Or so they think.

"YOU NEED A REFERRAL?" I'll never forget the time I asked a client of mine for a referral, and she was shocked to get the request. She said, "Gee, I see your trucks around *everywhere*." Translation: "I assume you guys are so busy that you couldn't possibly need referrals from me." I told her that our staff appreciates the career opportunities that come with growth, and assured her that we would be sure to take extra special care of anyone she referred to us.

Don't assume everyone knows you need or want referrals.

DO THE FOLLOWING EXERCISE. Think about your own home. Now think of someone who provides a professional service for your home. How many referrals do you go out of your way to solicit on your service provider's behalf, without being asked? (For most of you: probably not many.) Like the rest of us, your day is busy and your to-do list is long.

But what if your favorite vendor made it known that he or she wanted your help? Wouldn't you be more likely to offer a referral?

GET HELP FROM YOUR RAS! The reason you are more likely to help people who ask you for a referral has to do with a phenomenon associated with your RAS (pronounced 'raz'), also known as your *reticular activating system*. This is the part of your brain that filters out the millions of useless random impressions bombarding your brain—so you can focus on and accomplish your task at hand and your goals for the day.

Have you ever had the experience of buying a vehicle – say, a hybrid — and suddenly, you see hybrids everywhere? Your brain is now programmed to see these types of vehicles; while before, you never even noticed them.

When your vendor asks you for a referral and you agree to help him, your RAS then starts allowing the information to flow to your brain that will help you see referral opportunities for this vendor. You have, in effect, *programmed* your brain to look for referrals. (Thank you Ellen Ely for educating me on the RAS)

By the same token, this is the reason your customers don't necessarily bring you referrals – they aren't yet programmed to look for referrals for you!

Turn on your customer's RAS.
Let them know you want their referrals!

Can I assume that customers who don't complain are actively referring me?

This would be nice … but it is the wrong assumption to make.

DO A REALITY CHECK! Customers who don't complain may be happy … or they may not. They may be unhappy and simply not telling you.

Perhaps:

- There is a small issue bugging them.
- They don't want to bug you because they feel the issue is too small.
- It is not part of their personality to complain.
- They are stewing, waiting for you to ask them how everything is going, so they can finally let loose.

It's also possible that your customers have tried to tell you about the problems they're having, but for whatever reason, the message hasn't landed with you.

As a practical matter, if you are not getting the message that a client IS happy—you should assume that there's at least the chance of a problem. Assume there's something more you should be doing to improve the relationship. Assume that there's an issue somewhere that you haven't yet resolved to this person's satisfaction.

To address this:

1. Get back on the radar screen with clients you haven't heard from – and see what you can do for them.
2. Make sure you have a well functioning customer satisfaction survey in place.

Sometimes you just have to clean the cobwebs out of the relationship. People need to know that you care about them, and that you see them as more than just a paycheck.

ASKING BEGETS HAPPINESS. The ironic thing is, the act of asking people whether they're happy – will make them happy!

Should the head of our company ask our clients directly for referrals?

YES – if this person has a strong relationship with clients.

If, on the other hand, the client has a stronger relationship with a salesperson or account executive—then that salesperson or account executive should be the point person in charge of asking for and developing referrals.

I once asked a client for a referral when I shouldn't have. The client wanted his salesperson to make that request! The client wanted me, as the head of the company, to come around, listen to what was going on in his world, and chat — but NOT ask for referrals.

Perhaps my client somehow got the wrong message; perhaps he was worried that his salesperson was in trouble because the owner was calling, or perhaps he was wondering whether a change in personnel was in the works. In any event, he was not comfortable giving me the referral—he wanted to give referrals to the "key contact" – the salesperson. He wanted to see his salesperson succeed; he felt obliged to help his salesperson. (He did not feel obliged to help me.)

REFERRALS ARE PERSONAL. Clients often see them as something a particular individual earns — and it is an opportunity for a client to bestow a reward on that person.

If you're the owner of a fairly small company, and you have a tight relationship with the client, then yes, you are well advised to reach out and generate the referral.

My client says he wants to *keep us a secret.* How do we convince him to refer us?

When you mess up or miss your deadlines, clients will feel hesitant about referring you.

On the other hand, when you take care of your clients in a consistent, timely fashion without mistakes, your clients will feel confident referring you.

CAPACITY TO SPARE: The key, according to Dan Maki, Director of Property Care for GLEN GATE, based in Wilton, Connecticut, is to take care of your clients in a manner that sends the message that you have capacity to spare.

This way, they will feel comfortable referring you, without worrying about your ability to continue to service them at the high level they have come to enjoy. They know you will be able to follow through with them and make them look good for referring you.

PROMISE OF CARE: You will bolster the client's confidence by promising to take extra special care of anyone they refer to you. Of course, when you make this promise — you must mean it and follow through on it.

When you take care of your client's every wish, in what appears to be an *effortless* manner, your clients will actively refer you.

Even if you are super busy, you must appear to be super organized, so that you make it look easy, even when it isn't.

The better a job you do — by knowing your clients' expectations, keeping open lines of communication and anticipating individual needs — the more likely you will be to pull this off.

What's the final word on referrals? What should I focus on to increase referrals?

Focus on avoiding complacency. Never take people for granted. Keep caring about the little things.

Your clients will give you referrals – or stop giving you referrals – based on the little things you do for them consistently.

Here are some little things that will ALWAYS increase your chance of generating referrals:

- Answer your phone with passion – the passion that originally brought you into this business.

- Return your phone calls in a timely and caring manner.

- Be positive about everything. People are attracted to positive role models.

- Take pride in yourself. Dress well and groom yourself well, so that others will respect you.

- Treat your customer's property as you would treat your own property.. In fact, you may want to treat your customer's space better than you treat your own space. Let your pride show through. My happiest clients always comment on how much pride our employees take in their work.

- Keep your word. When you make a habit of following through on the promises you make to your customers, vendors and staff – you become worthy of receiving their referral.

- Think about the details – so clients and prospects don't have to. Manage the details for them, and they will give you referrals, because your work will stand out above everyone else's.

Not everyone will earn referrals. If you want to be among those who do, you must be willing to do the things that most people are not willing to do.

"The secret to attracting endless referrals, is to service your customer at such a high level that your competition would never consider copying you."

Jeffrey Scott

Use Peer Groups to Accelerate Your Success

Is your business on track for success?
Are you looking for new ways to increase profits?

THE LEADERS EDGE peer program will transform your business.

"This is the fresh set of eyes my company has needed to stay focused, on target, and profitable!"
— *Matt Kulp, Owner, Showcase Group*

"The Leaders Edge will help you tremendously to become a much more successful business owner."
— *Noel Ortiz, CEO, Great Outdoor Landscaping*

"The beauty of The Leaders Edge is that we exchange best practices, learn from each other and increase the profitability of our businesses."
— *Nathan Helder, President, Jan Gelderman Landscaping*

"For me, this is an opportunity to learn from the success of others … and avoid costly mistakes. Best of all, it all happens in a non-competitive environment
— *John Rennels, President, A Plus Lawn and Landscape*

Download a *free article* on how peer groups can help your business by visiting www.JeffreyScott.biz.

Learn more about The Leaders Edge by sending an e-mail to: Referrals@JeffreyScott.biz.

Book Jeffrey Scott to Speak!

Keynote talks and workshops

SALES SECRETS – Develop the weekly habits and strategies to generate and close more leads and get higher margins and a higher average sale.

THE REFERRAL ADVANTAGE – Learn how to ask for, earn, reward and inspire more customer and trade referrals! Learn how to grow your business by referral.

THE SECRETS OF BRANDING – Learn how to captivate your client, build your brand, and grow your business.

EVERYONE IS A MARKETING LEADER – Nothing happens until the phone rings. Learn the marketing fundamentals that everyone needs to master.

DRIVE YOUR PROFITS WITH AN OWNERS "DASHBOARD" – Every entrepreneur needs to focus on a small number of "profit drivers." Learn how to steer your company to more success.

NICHE MARKETING; BECOMING KNOWN AS THE EXPERT – Build market share by developing a niche and becoming known as the expert in your field.

ADVANCED PUBLIC RELATIONS – Learn the unwritten laws and creative principles that will create a buzz for your business and help it stand out in your community.

THE HIGH-END CLIENT – Attract and retain the affluent homeowner. Learn why they are different from you and me … and how to give them what they want.

FIVE KEYS TO KICK-BUTT CUSTOMER SERVICE – Delighting the customer is everyone's job! Learn what it takes to win clients for life.

PERSONAL SUCCESS – Build a personal brand and become an invaluable, irreplaceable resource in your company and community.

Looking to raise money for your association?

Contact us to find out about our innovative approaches to help you raise money.
Email us at Referrals@JeffreyScott.biz.

Landscape Success Systems

Implement better systems,
Improve people performance,
Make more money.

CEO COACHING – Helps owners to become better business leaders.

BUSINESS AUDITS – We look at systems, finances, management, the team, the product, and sales/marketing. We identify what's working, what's not, and what the fix is.

BUSINESS GROWTH COACHING– A tele-coaching format, to learn, apply and implement the key techniques and steps for growing your referrals, leads and sales.

SALES COACHING – Helps salespeople develop positive weekly and monthly habits, build relationships, and increase sales.

MARKETING AND GROWTH PLANNING – Identifies what you need to do, by when. Covers: creative solutions, systems, marketing collateral, branding, tracking and accountability.

CUSTOMER FOCUS GROUPS – Find out what they really want, and exactly what you have to do to attract and retain them. Stop guessing … and find out for sure!

STRATEGIC PLANNING AND RETREATS – Get the team motivated and on the same page. (For companies and associations.)

To find out more, visit www.JeffreyScott.biz or call 203 220-8931.